CONTENTS

Published by BBC Books,
a division of BBC Enterprises Limited,
Woodlands, 80 Wood Lane, London W12 0TT

First published 1994
© Gay Search 1994
Illustrations by Gill Tomblin
Photographs by Clive Nicholls and Anne Hyde
ISBN 0 563 37113 7

Set in 11/13 Plantin Light by Goodfellow & Egan Limited, Cambridge
Printed by Cambus Litho Ltd, East Kilbride
Bound by Hunter & Foulis Ltd, Edinburgh
Colour separations by Radstock Reproductions, Midsomer Norton
Jacket printed by Lawrence Allen Ltd, Weston-super-Mare

MORE FRONT GARDENS

NINE STUNNING NEW DESIGNS
TO TRANSFORM YOUR GARDEN

GAY SEARCH

BBC BOOKS

ACKNOWLEDGEMENTS

Our grateful thanks are due to the following companies and organizations for their generous help in transforming the gardens:

Building materials and equipment

Akzo Nobel Coatings Ltd.; Blue Circle Cement Ltd.; Borderstone Ltd.; Brandon Hire (Reading) plc.; Fleming and Co.; Forest Fencing Ltd.; General Decorating Supplies of Reading; Greenham Paving Ltd.; Alan Hadley Skips; Hall and Co.; Hall Aggregates (South East) Ltd.; Harcros Ltd.; Hicksons Timber Products Ltd.; Jewsons Timber Ltd.; Knightsbridge Garden Co. Ltd.; Larch-lap Ltd.; Marley Building Materials Ltd.; Marshalls of Halifax Ltd.; Ockley Building Products Ltd.; R M C Transite Ltd.; Redlands Aggregates Ltd.; Sadolins; Silverland Stone Ltd.; Town and Country Paving Ltd.; Valetta Surfacing Ltd; V.T. Plastics Ltd.

Accessories

Agriframes; Apta Terracotta Pottery; Aquacare Ltd.; Barlow Tyrie Ltd.; Black and Decker; Cannock Gates Ltd.; Concept Projects; Crown Paints; Duct & Access Covers Ltd.; The English Basket and Hurdle Company Ltd.; Flymo Ltd.; Hozelock Ltd.; Indian Ocean Trading Company Ltd.; Interploy Trading Co.; Lotus Water Garden Products Ltd.; Keep Able Tools; Naked Flame Ltd.; Olive Tree pots; Platipus Earth Anchoring Systems; Rako Products Ltd.; The Stewart Company; Simba Security Ltd.; Snapdragon Pots Ltd.; Spread Garden Supplies; Trade and DIY Products Ltd.; Whitchester Wood Design Ltd.; Christopher Winder Master Carpenters Ltd.; Woodlodge Products

Soil improvers, fertilizers and mulches

J. Arthur Bower's; Fisons Ltd.; Fleming & Co.; Gardenglow Cocoa Shells Ltd.; Greenvale Farm; Maskells Horticulture Ltd.; Sunshine of Africa Ltd.; Zeneca (formerly ICI) Garden Products

Plants

Barters' Farm Nurseries Ltd.; Burncoose and Southdown Nurseries; Country Gardens Ltd.; Cuckmere Valley Turf Farms; Derry Watkins Special Plants; Doorn Nurseries; Englefield Garden Centre; Goldbrook Plants; Greenholms Nurseries Ltd.; Hoo House Nursery; Kennedy's Garden Centres Ltd.; Kelways Nurseries; Kingstone Cottage Plants; Lingfield Nurseries; C.S. Lockyer Fuchsias; The Mead Nursery; Notcutts Ltd.; Poulshot Nurseries; PW Plants; The Otter Nursery; Rolawn Turf Growers Ltd.; Suttons Seeds Ltd.; Tendercare Nurseries Ltd.; Toad Hall Garden Centre (Henley-on-Thames) Ltd.; Waterwheel Nurseries.

Clothing

Falmers Jeans Ltd.; Millets Leisure Ltd.; Regatta Leisurewear.

Thanks also to Michael Twite Landscapes Ltd.; Reading Council; Kevin Wigginton; students from the Berkshire College of Horticulture and particular thanks are due to David Penny of the Berkshire College.

For a fact sheet containing details of all products and plants used, please send a cheque for £1.50 to Catalyst Television, Brook Green Studios, 186 Shepherds Bush Road, London W6 7LL.

INTRODUCTION

We decided to make the first television series of *Front Gardens* in 1992 because we felt it was clearly the great neglected area of gardening. Most of us have a front garden, very few of us know what to do with it and, although there are shelves full of books on garden design, hardly any of them has anything much to say about the patch out the front.

And when the series was broadcast it was immediately obvious that we had, indeed, struck a deep chord. Almost five and a half million viewers watched it each week, we had thousands of requests for our fact sheet – and sackfuls of letters from viewers offering their front gardens as raw material for the next series!

In the first few weeks after the first series went out, the garden owners got a hint at least of what it must be like to own a stately home. Although we had been deliberately vague about the precise locations to protect their privacy, some determined viewers set out to find them. The weekend after their programme went out, Paul and Gill Wallis reported traffic jams outside their sloping garden, with a fire engine drawing up at one point and the whole crew jumping out to have a proper look. The Sunday after the series finished, two ladies from Southampton, armed with the first *Front Gardens* book, set out to locate all the gardens. Several of the owners reported seeing them outside their new gardens and invited them in. The gardens that proved the most difficult to find were the four in the Victorian terrace. It is so well tucked away that even many locals don't know where it is. The only clue the intrepid ladies had was designer Jean Bishop's explanation that she'd created a diamond of green in one garden because the house was in the Jewellery Quarter. They found the area itself easily enough, but had no luck in locating the terrace. As it is still primarily a business area, it's virtually deserted on a Sunday, with no one around to ask, so the ladies were delighted when they finally spotted a man going into his office. They followed him in and asked if he knew where the gardens were. In one of those truly remarkable coincidences, he was probably the only man in the entire area that morning who *did* know – he was Norman Steemson, the cameraman who had shot the whole series.

In July 1993, the Victorian terrace gardens were recreated at the first *Gardeners' World Live!* show at the National Exhibition Centre in Birmingham. I was there the whole five days, and many people stopped to chat. Without doubt the question most visitors asked was whether the actual gardens were really that small, since they'd looked so much bigger on the screen. In fact, they were exactly the same size as the real thing – the camera always makes gardens look larger than they really are. A few also added that I too look much larger on the screen than I do in real life, though I wasn't quite sure how to take that!

It was also immensely gratifying to discover that people had been so inspired by the series that they had tackled their own front gardens as a direct result – and many of them had brought along the photographic evidence. In some cases they had copied a design almost exactly – the John Brookes garden with the gravel and the brick-edged circular beds was particularly popular – or they had adapted an idea. More often, though, what the series had done was make them realize that there was a lot they could do with their front garden, and they'd come up with a design of their own.

Many of them had scrapped the lawn, having seen that there were lots of other more attractive alternatives that didn't require such regular maintenance. We didn't set out to destroy the front lawns of Britain in the first series – honest! It just so happened that in all those gardens – except the cottage garden where the children needed a lawn to play on – the lawns served no useful purpose, and since they all looked terrible for a variety of different reasons (poor drainage, shade from trees, too small an area and so on) it seemed sensible to replace them with a more attractive mixture of easy-to-care-for hard landscaping, and soft planting.

But during the last eighteen months, since the first series was transmitted, the letters from viewers haven't stopped, many of them describing the problems they have with their own front gardens and commenting, 'You didn't tackle one like that last time!' And of course they were quite right. There were still a number of common problems that we didn't tackle – the garden sloping down to the house, for instance, the long thin garden, the garden that's an awkward shape . . . and hence *More Front Gardens*. Once again we've taken a number of ordinary gardens and with the help of six very talented designers transformed them, with the hope that in the process we will give you inspiration to tackle your own front garden and turn it into a source of delight, not just for you but for everyone who passes by.

Front Gardens *update*

When we did the final filming for the first series, in late August 1992, the plants had had just two months to grow. Luckily for us, it had rained almost continuously during those two months and everything had grown really well, but of course it takes anything from three to five years for a new garden to start looking its best, so it was but the blinking of an eye. We filmed several of the gardens for *Gardeners' World* one year later in August 1993, and the difference was already quite remarkable, but by summer 1994, when the photographs were taken for this book, the transformation was even more astonishing. And it's proof for the surprising number of cynics in this world that the gardens are still there, and that we hadn't, as some of them suspected, arrived with huge vans the day after filming was finished and taken everything away!

The Victorian terrace

At No 11, all the herbs we'd planted were spilling on to the path, and much of the maintenance Cathy Harper had had to do was cutting back when it all became too much. The lavenders had grown together to form a large clump against which you brush as you walk into the garden, and the slightly tender germander (*Teucrium fruticans*) with its soft grey leaves and powder-blue flowers was thriving, growing into the one planted on the other side of the railings in No 10, linking the two in the way that designer Jean Bishop had intended. Through the railings, Cathy had planted sweet peas in soft pinks, blues and creams which looked really pretty. The climbers on the walls – the clematis by the door, the honeysuckle and the quince we'd planted against the wall at the end of the terrace – were all growing well. Cathy still loves her garden though she had to rent the house out for a year while she was working abroad, and left her tenant very detailed instructions for the care of the garden.

Next door, Cindy Etheridge's garden looked just as good. The roses – the buff-yellow 'Gloire de Dijon', the deep pink 'Reine Victoria' and 'Climbing Iceberg' – had reached the top of the black metal obelisks, and were full of flower. Beneath them, the ground-cover plants had really begun to grow together and form the carpets of attractive foliage which Jean had intended – the rich purple of *Heuchera* 'Palace Purple' and the silver of *Cerastium alpinum* – while the spiky plants, like the variegated sisyrinchiums and the smoky pink, cream and purple phormiums, had started to form impressive-looking

In their third summer, all four gardens are beginning to look really mature. The ivies at Number 8 (*far left*) have scrambled all over the rockery and the sides of the seat, while Number 9 (*left*) has the tapestry of green its owners wanted.

Even without the pots (in store while the owner was abroad) the strong bones and soft planting in Number 11 (*left*) mean it still looks very good. The climbing roses, 'Reine Victoria', 'Gloire de Dijon' and 'Cl. Iceberg' in Number 10 (*above*) have covered the obelisks with flowers.

11

clumps. A couple of the lavenders weren't doing too well, so they were replaced.

In the third garden, No 9, where Jean Bishop had set out to create a textured tapestry of different greens, for brothers Richard and Andrew Lynch, she had virtually succeeded in her aim. The diamond of green – created with the very low-growing, powerfully scented Corsican mint (*Mentha requienii*) – had run into problems by June 1994. Probably as a result of a very wet winter, and a wet, cold spring, much of it had rotted away and would have to be replaced with something like ornamental grasses or ivy.

Almost all the evergreen shrubs were thriving – the mahonia, the soft juniper (*Juniperus sabina* 'Tamariscifolia'), the box-leaved honeysuckle (*Lonicera pileata*), the small Japanese holly (*Ilex crenata* 'Convexa') – and although the *Fatshedera* in the corner appeared to have succumbed the first winter, it had produced strong new growth by the following spring. The snowy mespilus (*Amelanchier canadensis*) was also looking good – its brilliant autumn colour much appreciated by everyone in the terrace.

By the end of its third year, the garden of No 8 was really looking as Jean had intended with the different, small-leaved ivies now scrambling over the rockery under the window, the York stone in the sunken garden and the L-shaped stone seat. The small, purple-leaved *Viola labradorica* had seeded itself everywhere and was growing all along the rope-twist edging tiles and in any gaps between the slabs. The one gap in the garden Tina Rozsas wanted to fill was a terracotta pot with some ivy growing happily enough in it. She also wanted something with purple or mauve flowers throughout the summer, so we planted a small hebe, *H.* 'Margret', which has pale mauve flowers that fade to white as they mature.

The new estate

Although everything grew remarkably well in all our gardens during their first summer, the plants in our communal garden for a pair of small modern semis did best of all. It may have been to do with the fact that the new large raised area provided the excellent drainage which sun-loving plants need, or with the woven membrane through which we planted, keeping the moisture in and the weeds down – we didn't know. Whatever the explanation, though, it was hard to believe that the garden had only been planted two months earlier. When we filmed the garden again the following year, the remarkably rapid rate of growth had been maintained. Indeed, Annette and Glenn Wright had had to remove a few of the plants on their side and find them new homes.

The lovely rose, *Rosa chinensis* 'Mutabilis', with flame-coloured buds that open into coppery-yellow flowers, then turn a coppery pink and finally crimson ('Mutabilis' means 'changing' – see, there *is* a point to these Latin names!), was proving a stunning focal point in the centre of the garden, flowering right through the summer and well into the autumn. On the walls, the climbers had really started to do their job. The white rose 'Albéric Barbier' was growing incredibly well by summer 94 and all the clematis, from the spring-flowering *C. alpina* 'Helsingborg' and the late summer-flowering *C. rehderiana* 'Royal Velours' to the large-flowered hybrids, like the soft blue 'Lasurstern', provided, as planned, the longest possible season of interest.

In the first year we'd planted the cup-and-saucer vine (*Cobaea scandens*) but it went in rather late and there was so little sun in the latter part of the summer that it didn't flower that year. Glenn sowed seed in the greenhouse the following spring, put the plants out in late May and that summer it reached about 3.8m (12ft) in height and produced its curious greeny-white and deep mauve cup-and-saucer-like flowers. Annette and Glenn had loved the free-flowering, pale yellow *Argyranthemum* 'Jamaica Primrose', which formed an enormous clump at the bottom of their steps. It isn't reliably hardy, so they'd taken cuttings each year to overwinter in the greenhouse so they had healthy new plants each summer.

There were, if anything, even more pots on the steps, with small evergreen shrubs like euonymus and skimmia for winter interest and tender fuchsias, as well as pots simply crammed with annuals like petunias and busy Lizzies.

The only addition was a few circular cement paving stones strategically placed in among the chippings, to make them slightly easier to walk on.

Next door, Steve and Lorraine Everitt had found their side of the garden very easy to look after, as requested, with just the odd bit of snipping back needed here and there.

The cottage garden

By the end of the second summer Karen and Andy O'Neill's garden looked as if it had always been there. Although there seemed to be a predominance of hard landscaping when it was first planted, the herbaceous perennials, like *Geranium sanguineum striatum*, *G.* 'Russell Prichard', catmint (*Nepeta fassenii*) and lady's mantle (*Alchemilla mollis*), very soon spilled over on to the paving, softening its impact considerably. In the bed to the right of the path, the silver weeping pear (*Pyrus salicifolia* 'Pendula') started to fill out and screen the more modern house extension from the gate. Beneath it, where the courgettes had been planted the first summer, they'd planted a *Fatsia japonica* because it

In the cottage garden (*left*) much of the hard landscaping is now hidden under plants like lady's mantle, catmint and hardy geraniums, while honeysuckle and the deep pink rose 'Lavinia' have covered the arch over the gate.

Everything in the new estate garden (*below*) has grown so well that it's hard to see the serpentine retaining wall now beneath the purple sage, the campanula and the carpeting *Persicaria* 'Dimity' cascading over it.

has rather similar-shaped leaves and of course is evergreen. The grasses – both the golden oat grass (*Stipa gigantea*) and the curious, horizontally striped *Miscanthus sinensis* 'Zebrinus' – did particularly well, the former throwing up plumes of tiny flowers well over 2m (6ft) high.

The play area with the built-in sandpit was very successful, and stood up well to quite a bashing from Emily, now five, and Abigail, a baby in arms when we first met her and now an energetic three.

Under the bow windows at the front of the cottage, the two new beds, curved to follow the lines of the windows, were looking very good indeed. Cottage garden plants such as lupins, foxgloves (like the lovely strawberry-sorbet-coloured *Digitalis* × *mertonensis*), and the old, single-flowered hollyhocks which reached the bedroom windows the second summer, had filled out and, along with more modern varieties of old plants like *Lavatera* 'Barnsley', created the desired jumbly effect. The roses and honeysuckle over the white arch above the gate had reached the top. 'Phyllis Bide', a rambler with small, pink-tinged, buff flowers which we'd planted to grow up the black trellis by the front door, had done its job just as effectively. Perhaps the one disappointment in the garden had been the new ground-cover rose in the 'County' series – 'Sussex'. Although it is probably the most attractive of all with coppery peach-apricot flowers and glossy bronze-green leaves, it is the most prone to blackspot, and in a wet summer like that of 93 the disease really thrives. The second year, it clobbered both groups of 'Sussex' on either side of the path so badly that by the end of the summer they had barely a leaf left on them. The only solution was a very radical haircut, a spraying with benomyl and crossed fingers through the winter. It seemed to pay off. The following spring, they looked healthy enough and when we photographed the garden again in the summer of 1994 they were looking very good.

The 1930s semi

What a difference even a year makes! The garden designed by John Brookes included a large new curved bed with lots of shrubs, and since they were relatively small when they went in it was inevitable that the garden looked a bit sparse when it was finished in the summer of 92. When we planted it, many of the shrubs were smaller than the perennials, but fifteen months on, when we went back to film, they had begun to reach their proper proportions. As recommended, Bryan and Jenny Pullinger had cut back the lovely white. hydrangea (*H. arborescens* 'Annabelle') really hard the first autumn after planting, and had been rewarded with very strong, bushy growth the following year, well able to support the heavy heads of flower.

Of the evergreens – or rather 'evergolds' in most instances – the shrubby honeysuckle (*Lonicera nitida* 'Baggesen's Gold'), the Japanese holly (*Ilex crenata* 'Golden Gem') and the spindles (*Euonymus fortunei* 'Emerald 'n' Gold' and *E. japonicus*) to the left of the drive had all grown well and provided welcome splashes of gold in the winter. Perhaps the most spectacular plant was what the Pullingers christened 'the Triffid' – the *Verbascum olympicum*, which in the second summer produced tall stems of felty grey leaves and yellow flowers almost 3m (10ft) high, which waved about in the wind like wiry, ghostly arms. Since it's biennial, it died at the end of the second summer, and hadn't appeared to self-seed, so Bryan and Jenny replaced it with two *Choisya ternata* 'Sundance', to bulk out the existing group.

In his original plan, John Brookes had wanted to fill one of the two brick-edged circles in the gravel with massed blue ageratums, but by the time we came to plant the garden at the end of June it was too late and we couldn't find any anywhere. In the second year, though, Bryan and Jenny did plant them and against the gold foliage behind, next to the lime-yellow flowers of the self-seeded alchemillas in the gravel, they looked stunning. In the borders the overall colour scheme of gold, blue and white – penstemons, the striking aster, *A. frikartii* 'Mönch', and *Liriope muscari* providing the blue, with Japanese anemones and agapanthus providing the white – worked extremely well. The Pullingers picked up the blue and yellow colour scheme in the hanging baskets, too, using pale blue trailing lobelia, deeper blue scaevola and the yellow-flowered bidens – an excellent plant for containers with its trailing habit, daisy-like flowers all summer long and feathery foliage.

The one failure had been with a hellebore (*H. corsicus*), one of three planted in the raised bed created by the circular wall around the lovely multi-stemmed silver birch. It had died in the first winter, and had been replaced by the garden centre which supplied it. But by the end of the second summer, its replacement was dying too. It likes free-draining but rich soil that doesn't dry out too much, so the most likely explanation was that, as there was quite a lot of rubble under the raised bed, the soil in that particular spot was just too shallow and too dry for it. By the beginning of the third season, though, the other two were growing so well, spreading to about three times their original width, that Bryan and Jenny didn't bother to replace it.

Despite dire warnings that the local cat population would turn the gravelled area into a large litter tray, that simply didn't happen. A few annual weeds seeded themselves in the gravel, but no perennial weeds managed to fight their way through the well-compacted layer of hard core underneath. Apart from the odd instance of local children picking up handfuls of gravel and throwing it around, there were no problems with it at all. In fact the Pullingers were so pleased with the gravel that they've used it in the back garden in a very shady area under an old apple tree where very little would grow. All in all they were thrilled with the garden and, as the plants rapidly matured, even the few neighbours who hadn't been too keen initially were won over.

The sloping garden

Like the 1930s semi, this garden also looked a bit stark after the plants went in, and the banks of zigzagged railway sleepers, used to contain the slope from the bungalow to the road, did dominate rather. But by the end of the following summer there was already a marked difference, as plants like ivies began to tumble down over the sleepers, or grow up above them like the tall crimson-leafed berberis 'Red Pillar' to break up and soften the very strong horizontal lines. The two groups of *Cistus* × *corbariensis*, one of the hardier cistuses, planted either side of what became known as Postman Pat's path – the line of stepping stones through the garden following the postman's existing 'desire line' – had grown well and by the third summer had joined up to form a long clump. Plants growing in the gravel, such as the thymes and the blue grasses, like *Helictotrichon sempervirens*, had also started to spread, so the gravel wasn't quite so dominant either. The plants in the pools had gone berserk – it was just as well that we'd planted cool green and white striped gardener's garters (*Phalaris arundinacea* 'Picta') and the grass-like rush (*Acorus gramineus*) in special plastic baskets to contain their more rapacious tendencies – and the sound of water flowing gently over the slate lip was still a great source of calm.

Having seen the garden through all four seasons, Paul and Gill Wallis had decided that they wanted a bit more winter colour, and so had planted a group of hellebores (*H. corsicus*) and a group of dwarf conifers like *Picea glauca* 'Alberta Globe' and *Thuja plicata* 'Stoneham Gold' on the left of the garden, beyond the pool. To help soften the impact of the sleepers even more, they'd planted a japonica (*Chaenomeles*) and a firethorn (*Pyracantha*) and trained them against the wood. They'd also added some French lavender (*L. stoechas*) by the drive and some ferns, like the lovely painted Japanese fern (*Athyrium niponicum* 'Pictum').

There had been a couple of failures. The bright golden, cut-leaved elder (*Sambucus racemosa* 'Plumosa Aurea') had not looked at all well the second spring, with the leaves turning brown and dropping off. Paul moved it to the back garden where it soon recovered. This suggests that the exposed, north-east-facing front garden was just too cold and windy for it. In its place Paul and Gill planted a golden larch (*Pseudolarix*

The proper balance between hard landscaping and planting has been reached in the 1930s semi garden (*left*), though the strong, simple bones of John Brookes's design are still very clear.

In the low maintenance garden, too (*left*), the plants are softening the hard lines of the garden itself and of the new porch.

The stark lines of the railway sleepers no longer dominate the sloping garden (*right and below*) as they did when it was just finished, and the plants in the gravel have spread to soften its appearance, too.

amabilis), a deciduous conifer whose fresh green leaves turn bright golden-orange in the autumn. It will eventually make a largish tree – 10–12m (33–40ft) tall – so they will need to keep an eye on it and take it out before it gets too big.

The only other failure was one of the group of *Viburnum davidii* to the left of the front door, which had died. The others around it were thriving, so the likely explanation was that this particular one had been planted just too close to the bungalow walls, so that it didn't get enough water and died of drought. In its place, the Wallises had planted a rose, 'Golden Showers', to match the one on the other side of the door, and had taken care to plant it a good 30cm (12in) away from the wall, where the soil wasn't too dry. The garden had proved extremely easy to look after, with only a few weeds poking through the gravel, but Paul and Gill were still so thrilled with their garden that they loved every minute they spent pottering about in it.

The low-maintenance garden

Beryl Whitten's front garden – 144 concrete paving slabs and the odd dandelion growing in the cracks – had been so bleak when we started work on it that anything we did was bound to be a huge improvement. In fact the finished result, designed by Robin Williams, was really lovely, and even after just a few months the new raised area, on to which Beryl could walk out from her front door *and* tend at waist height from the pavement, looked extremely good. The porch, designed to emphasize the front door in an otherwise blank frontage, did look very new at first but, a couple of years on, the 'Golden Showers' rose had grown up through the trellis and softened its appearance considerably. On the trellis to the left of the garage, the soft pink *Clematis montana* 'Elizabeth' was growing very well, and attracted many admiring comments when it was in full flower in the spring. The two small trees we planted – snowy mespilus (*Amelanchier canadensis*) and the small maple (*Acer henryi*) – were both growing well, despite the latter being blown over by a particularly fierce gale the first autumn. The snowy mespilus, particularly in spring when it is in full flower, gave Beryl enormous pleasure and she spent hours at her front-room window just gazing out at it.

By the end of the second summer, the catmint (*Nepeta mussinii*) planted between the new wall and the actual front boundary of the garden had grown together to form a low hedge, and seemed to have survived the attentions of both the local cats – and dogs! The lavenders planted on the left-hand boundary had also done well on the whole, although a couple of plants closest to the pavement had needed to be replaced the second year. The soil in that trench was very poor and particularly shallow right by the pavement, so we tried feeding the plants with pelleted chicken manure, and they seemed to perk up.

The clump of violas (*V.* 'Ardross Gem') hadn't thrived despite being replaced once, although they are certainly hardy enough for an exposed spot like that. In spring 1994 Beryl replaced them with the evergreen carpeter *Ajuga reptans* 'Braunherz', with very glossy purple-bronze leaves and spikes of vivid blue flowers in early summer.

Almost all the other shrubs and perennials had grown very well. The lovely *Coreopsis verticillata* 'Moonbeam', with its pale yellow daisy flowers and fresh green dill-like foliage, had done a wonderful job in the newly planted garden of softening both the large boulders placed in a group, and the quarter-standard light we had installed. So although they hadn't survived the first particularly cold winter, Beryl had loved them so much she replaced them the following year. The poached-egg plant (*Limnanthes douglasii*), the extremely useful low-growing annual with white and yellow flowers and fern-like foliage, had seeded itself from year to year, even flowering through the winter in 94, and filling in the ever-decreasing gaps as the permanent planting filled out. In the centre of the gravel, the saxifragas really romped away, so much so that Beryl had to dig them up and divide them.

The only real disaster happened one night in February 94, when someone stole Beryl's favourite conifer, the little pine (*Pinus nigra laricio* 'Moseri'). Several neighbours also lost specimen shrubs the same night and, according to the local police, they would almost certainly have been sold at a car boot sale. As a precaution, Beryl decided to dig up another favourite, the very slow-growing golden yew (*Taxus baccata* 'Standishii') and keep it in a pot, along with the replacement *Pinus nigra laricio* 'Moseri', until the spate of thefts had passed. That apart, the garden has continued to give her great pleasure.

THE AWKWARD-SHAPED GARDEN

While most front gardens are rectangular, by no means all are, and irregular shapes can create all sorts of design problems. Our problem garden was on a council estate, started four years ago and completed in the summer of 1993.

Learie and Louise Hampden and their three children Morgan, 13, Laura, 10, and Nathan, 5, were allocated the end house in their particular close, with a much larger-than-average front garden 14.5 × 9.5m (48 × 30ft). It was simply the luck of the draw but, as it happens, Louise is an enthusiastic gardener and, having done a horticulture course at the local agricultural college, she is now studying garden design. Although it was clear from a quick look round the garden that Louise was keen and knowledgeable, even she hadn't been able to come up with a way of making the garden work as a whole. That's not surprising, since it was not without its problems. As you walked into the garden, it was much wider than it was deep and your eye went straight to the fence running the width of the garden. Although there was a 2m (6ft) high wall to the left of the entrance, the other side had only a low railing fence, so it was wide open to the prevailing wind from the south-west, which whistled into the garden bringing litter from the estate with it. The wind also knocked the plants about and dried out the leaves, turning them brown round the edges.

The estate was built on a flood plain, so the soil was silty. Silt shares many of the same problems and properties as clay, only it's smooth and silky to touch rather than sticky. Like clay, it can become airless, water-logged and heavy to work when it's wet and it tends to be cold as well, which means that plants grown from seed either take an age to germinate or don't germinate at all. When it dries out it 'caps' – forms a hard crust – so any seeds that have managed to germinate find it very hard to push their way through.

The good news is that soils like this are usually rich in nutrients, and the fact that they are water-retentive means they don't dry out as quickly as lighter soils in case of drought. Once the drainage has been improved, silt will grow very good plants indeed.

Testing for the acidity of the soil was part of Louise's horticulture course, so she already knew that the soil was just about neutral, meaning that most plants, apart from a few real acid-lovers like rhododendrons, would thrive. Beyond the long fence on the far side of the garden was part-wasteland, part-nature reserve. The plus was that the garden was visited by lots of wildlife. The minus was that perennial weeds like couch grass which rampaged unchecked out there came creeping in under the fence.

As an incorrigible, self-confessed 'plant-watcher', what Louise wanted from her front garden was a framework within which to grow a wide range of plants to reflect the seasons and give her something attractive to look at all through the year. She had considered getting rid of the lawn, which was a chore to cut and never looked good, to provide more space in which to indulge her hobby.

While the plants are her primary interest, she also wanted the garden to be an attractive space in its own right, to welcome people to the house, and somewhere to sit in warm weather to watch the children playing in the close.

Learie, who sees his role in the garden primarily as the muscle, wanted a garden that made you go 'Wow!' when you walked into it. As for colours, he liked the brighter shades in the spectrum – reds and yellows particularly – while Louise liked all colours if used carefully in the right combinations, though, if she were forced to choose, she would go for the pastels rather than the primaries.

The designer we invited to work on Louise's garden, Dan Pearson, was a kindred spirit. Although he is one of the most original garden designers around, both his training at the RHS garden at Wisley and at the Royal Botanical Gardens, Kew, and his own inclination mean that plants have always had pride of place in his work.

The design

The first thing Dan bore in mind was the house itself and the estate around it because, to work well, the design had to be in context with both. That indicated that the hard landscaping should be quite simple – and also cheap, since a growing family meant there wasn't much cash to spare. The second major factor was Louise's passion for plants, so he wanted to provide as large a space for them as possible. He therefore planned to provide the interest and the drama with plants, not hard landscaping.

He felt the existing path of huge concrete slabs to the front door sliced across at a very ugly angle, but since regular visitors will always take the shortest possible route, he was stuck with its position. So he softened it a lot by getting rid of the slabs and using paviours that blended with the house bricks, by curving the new path and 'fraying' the edges into the border.

To solve the problem of the awkward shape, Dan created a large, brick-edged circle of gravel in the centre of the garden, which immediately took your eye away from both the odd layout and the wide expanses of fence. He chose a circle because it's such a strong, simple shape, and he believes that simplicity is the key. If he has three ideas, he immediately whittles them down to one, and then makes it as big and bold as possible. Certainly the circle looked very dominant in the newly built, unplanted garden, but then Dan's gardens are always so heavily planted that they need big 'bones' to balance the planting. His paths are always at least a metre wide because once the plants are in on either side, there is rarely more than 30cm (12in) of walking space left in the middle. Certainly, once the circle was planted according to the plan, only about half the original area of gravel would be visible. Even without a plant in it, Louise loved the new layout, and was astonished at how much lighter the inside of the house was in the morning, with the light bouncing off the gravel.

Dan liked the existing fences, which had weathered to an attractive silvery brown, though he couldn't understand why the long fence had been put in the wrong way round, with the back facing into the garden. So he decided to fix trellis on that section of fence – off-the-peg panels of ordinary small-squared trellis, stained a lovely deep blue shade called 'Iris' – which would provide support for the climbers he was going to plant and give an interesting three-dimensional effect until they had covered it entirely. When that happens, the eye will move from the circle to the planting and come to rest on the line of trees beyond, not really registering the boundaries at all.

He also included a couple of his jokey hallmarks. The first was a box armchair in which you can sit quite comfortably. It consists of a metal framework through which box is grown and then clipped to shape as it fills the space. The second was a tall spiral of ivy which marks the entrance to the garden and moves in the wind.

On the south-facing fence Dan sited a bench seat with an arbour above it to play host to a range of climbing plants. Originally he thought of metal to match the armchair but the cost ruled it out, so instead he opted for a very chunky DIY bench made from two slices of telegraph pole for the legs and a planed plank bolted to them for the seat. To create a feeling of enclosure, he suggested drilling a series of holes 10cm (4in) apart along the back to take 2m (6ft) hazel bean poles, which would be pushed into the soil for support and up which we would grow climbers.

The only other feature in the garden is a huge, greyish-brown glazed Thai pot, a fat,

The awkward-shaped garden in its former state – the photograph (*left*) has been taken from the right of the front door – looks very bland and uninteresting. Three months later the garden – the photograph (*below*) taken from over the garden wall – looks stunning with the gravel circle a riot of hot, strong colours and the rest of the planting filling out very quickly.

squat, rough Ali Baba shape, easily large enough for an adult to hide in. It cost about £90 – not cheap but a fraction of what you would pay for terracotta and, again, it fits in with Dan's philosophy of 'the bigger the better'. It has much more impact than two or three smaller pots, which would cost as much, you can grow virtually anything in it, from a tree downwards, it will need watering less often, and it's extremely unlikely to get stolen. Even unplanted, it was a massive, dramatic sculptural shape to divert the eye from the awkward-shaped space and deliver more of the 'Wow!' factor. At Dan's suggestion, we planted it with a mixture of deep purple petunias and ruby chard.

Building the garden

Once Dan had decided which of the old plants he wanted to use in the new scheme – the flowering purple-leaved plum (*Prunus pissardii* 'Nigra'), hellebores, laurustinus (*Viburnum tinus*), the climbing rose, 'Ena Harkness' on the wall – we dug up the rest and found them new homes.

The next thing to do was to kill off the grass with a systemic weedkiller containing glyphosate. It takes a couple of weeks to work but it kills the whole plant, not just the top growth, so there is no problem with regrowth. It also becomes inactive on contact with the soil, so there is no danger at all to soil organisms or to new plants.

Once the grass was dead, we dug it in because it provides valuable organic matter. To cope with the problems of the silty soil, we dug in even more bulky organic matter (composted bark in this instance, though well-rotted manure, spent hops, garden compost or composted straw would have done as well) and horticultural grit – about a bucketful of each to the square metre – to open up the soil, and improve both the drainage and the fertility.

Over by the long fence, couch grass growing in underneath from the waste ground next door had been a real problem. The glyphosate weedkiller had killed off the visible couch and, as we dug it over, we pulled out any bits of root we saw, but it was still there, on the other side of the fence, just waiting to creep under and colonize the well-cultivated soil we had prepared. So we dug a trench along the bottom of the fence, nailed strips of old, heavy-duty black polythene about 25cm (10in) deep to the gravel board, and refilled the trench with soil. You couldn't see the polythene at all, but it was there as a physical barrier against the invading couch.

Because the design of the garden was deliberately simple, and the materials chosen both cheap and designed for DIY, Louise and Learie were able to do much of the work themselves, laying the paving on a bed of sand and the gravel – except on the two areas inside the brick edging where there was to be planting – on a layer of compacted roadstone to keep the weeds at bay. Solving the various problems caused by the wind wasn't easy. To create some protection for the more vulnerable plants Dan formed a windbreak using other, tougher plants.

Planting

In the bed most exposed to the wind, he planted shrubs like *Elaeagnus angustifolia* 'Caspica' (also sold as *E. a.* 'Quicksilver'), which is very tough but also very elegant with its long, slender, silvery leaves that shimmer in the wind. It looks a bit like the silver-leaved pear, but is more useful in a situation like this because it's so quick-growing. Its open habit means that its branches sway with the wind and, while they provide some privacy they also allow Louise to keep an eye on the children playing in the close. It has small lime-green flowers with the most delicious scent in summer. With it, Dan planted another toughie, *Rosa glauca (R. rubrifolia* as was), grown primarily for its wonderful smoky purple-grey foliage. Its graceful arching stems look very attractive moving in the wind.

Dan then filled the rest of that corner bed with a deep swathe of Old English lavender (*Lavandula angustifolia*), the tallest variety, to provide a bit more protection from the wind than the smaller ones. Along with the elaeagnus flowers, the lavender would scent the short journey to the front door, too. In the front, as an edging, there's the hummock-forming hardy geranium, bloody cranesbill (*G. sanguineum*), with saucer-shaped magenta flowers all summer, and an iris whose name – 'Deep Black' – indicates its colour very plainly.

At the entrance, Dan put a spiral of the lovely glossy deep green Irish ivy (*Hedera hibernica*). He used a plant 2m (6ft) high and trained it round and round a very stout wire frame with four long prongs which were pushed deep into the soil. It's an idea that's relatively easy to copy, either with a ready-made metal topiary frame (although the central support most of them have means it won't be as flexible as ours), or with one you get the local blacksmith or metalwork shop to make up for you. If you're competent and reasonably strong, you could make one yourself.

What dictated Dan's thinking about the planting generally was the fact that Louise is an avid plant collector, so he wanted a bold, definite colour scheme, using large areas of the same colour – a large sweep of blue covering most of one fence and a good bit of another, for example, using the Chilean potato-vine (*Solanum crispum* 'Glasnevin') and the good old purple clematis 'Jackmanii' together – to create a canvas for Louise to work on in the future. For the same reason, he used a wide range of colours. If he'd gone for just silvers, whites and pale pinks, say, it would have made it difficult for Louise to add in any little jewels that she acquired. For Learie, there are shots of brilliant colour – *Monarda* 'Cambridge Scarlet', for example, *Potentilla* 'Gibson's Scarlet', *Crocosmia* 'Lucifer' and bright yellow coneflower (*Rudbeckia fulgida deamii*) – usually planted against darker smokier colours, like the black-stemmed bamboo (*Phyllostachys nigra*), *Buddleia davidii* 'Black Knight' and bronze fennel (*Foeniculum vulgare* 'Purpureum'). Dan likes to weave his colours, with drifts moving through each other, rather than in clumps arranged side by side, and have them occurring again in other parts of the garden.

Foliage colour is very important too, not just for its own long-lasting qualities but for weaving contrasting flower colours together. He uses silver and smoky purple foliage, for example, as a link between cerise and magenta flowers on one side of the path and yellow flowers on the other side – pale yellow at first with Jerusalem sage (*Phlomis fruticosa*) and *Coreopsis verticillata* 'Moonbeam', then moving into the egg-yolk-yellow flowers of pineapple broom (*Cytisus battandieri*), and Spanish broom (*Spartium junceum*). Pineapple broom is normally trained on a sunny wall or fence but, in that very sheltered sunny corner, Dan thought it would do well as a free-standing shrub.

Moving down the long fence from left to right, the foliage colour changes from silver to green. By the time you reach the sheltered north-facing corner, the emphasis is on contrasts in foliage texture, shape and colour – green and gold – with the plain gold dogwood *Cornus alba* 'Aurea', the stunning Japanese angelica tree (*Aralia elata*) and dark green laurustinus (*Viburnum tinus*). That's true of the climbers too – the plain green Persian ivy (*Hedera colchica*) and the golden hop (*Humulus lupulus* 'Aureus') which looks superb against the dark blue trellis, with the late-flowering yellow clematis *C. orientalis* 'Bill Mackenzie' scrambling through them and over the gate through to the back garden.

Dan always tries to find one or two real gems for his gardens, and in this instance he had found a rose, 'Louis XIV', about which he was very excited. It's a small China rose, with masses of small, scented, deep red – almost black – semi-double flowers throughout the summer. With it, he planted the deep red day lily, *Hemerocallis* 'Stafford'.

In the small shady bed to the left of the front door, he added to Louise's hellebore collection with some more *H. foetidus*, and other spring-flowering woodland plants like Solomon's seal (*Polygonatum* × *hybridum*) and lungwort (*Pulmonaria saccharata*).

The shape and texture of foliage are as important as its colour in Dan's scheme, and he has used two very dramatic, fast-growing foliage plants for guaranteed 'Wow!' factor – the honeybush (*Melianthus major*), which has huge jagged blue-grey leaves, and the Japanese angelica tree which has vaguely similar leaves but very dark green this time. It

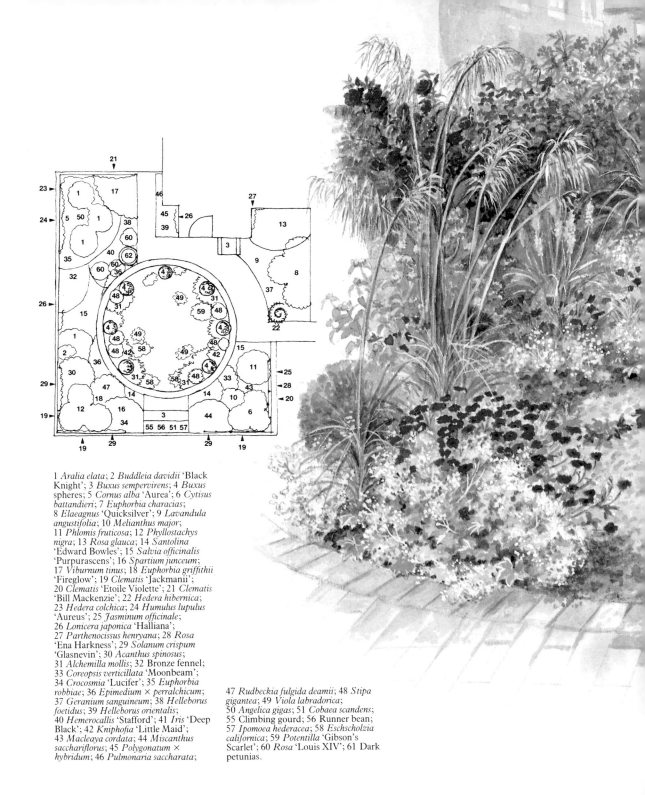

1 *Aralia elata*; 2 *Buddleia davidii* 'Black Knight'; 3 *Buxus sempervirens*; 4 *Buxus* spheres; 5 *Cornus alba* 'Aurea'; 6 *Cytisus battandieri*; 7 *Euphorbia characias*; 8 *Elaeagnus* 'Quicksilver'; 9 *Lavandula angustifolia*; 10 *Melianthus major*; 11 *Phlomis fruticosa*; 12 *Phyllostachys nigra*; 13 *Rosa glauca*; 14 *Santolina* 'Edward Bowles'; 15 *Salvia officinalis* 'Purpurascens'; 16 *Spartium junceum*; 17 *Viburnum tinus*; 18 *Euphorbia griffithii* 'Fireglow'; 19 *Clematis* 'Jackmanii'; 20 *Clematis* 'Etoile Violette'; 21 *Clematis* 'Bill Mackenzie'; 22 *Hedera hibernica*; 23 *Hedera colchica*; 24 *Humulus lupulus* 'Aureus'; 25 *Jasminum officinale*; 26 *Lonicera japonica* 'Halliana'; 27 *Parthenocissus henryana*; 28 *Rosa* 'Ena Harkness'; 29 *Solanum crispum* 'Glasnevin'; 30 *Acanthus spinosus*; 31 *Alchemilla mollis*; 32 Bronze fennel; 33 *Coreopsis verticillata* 'Moonbeam'; 34 *Crocosmia* 'Lucifer'; 35 *Euphorbia robbiae*; 36 *Epimedium* × *perralchicum*; 37 *Geranium sanguineum*; 38 *Helleborus foetidus*; 39 *Helleborus orientalis*; 40 *Hemerocallis* 'Stafford'; 41 *Iris* 'Deep Black'; 42 *Kniphofia* 'Little Maid'; 43 *Macleaya cordata*; 44 *Miscanthus sacchariflorus*; 45 *Polygonatum* × *hybridum*; 46 *Pulmonaria saccharata*;

47 *Rudbeckia fulgida deamii*; 48 *Stipa gigantea*; 49 *Viola labradorica*; 50 *Angelica gigas*; 51 *Cobaea scandens*; 55 Climbing gourd; 56 Runner bean; 57 *Ipomoea hederacea*; 58 *Eschscholzia californica*; 59 *Potentilla* 'Gibson's Scarlet'; 60 *Rosa* 'Louis XIV'; 61 Dark petunias.

**The awkward-shaped garden
in five years' time**

also has clusters of small white flowers in late summer/early autumn, and very interesting twisted stems which look good in winter. It is much hardier than the melianthus, which may well send up new shoots from the base in spring if it does get clobbered by the frost.

There is a fair proportion of evergreens too, cleverly spaced throughout the garden – the tall, very elegant blue-black stems of the bamboo (*Phyllostachys nigra*), which picks up the colour of the trellis to perfection, *Viburnum tinus*, Japanese honeysuckle (*Lonicera japonica* 'Halliana') and ivy on the fences, cotton lavender (*Santolina*) and clipped box balls – to provide some winter interest wherever you look.

Near the bench, scent is important, so there's the pineapple broom for early summer, and the honeysuckle, Spanish broom and jasmine (*Jasminum officinale*) for mid-summer onwards. Instead of traditional climbers over the arbour, Dan chose to use vegetables – runner beans and climbing gourds (*Cucurbita*) – and also used others, like ruby chard and red oak-leaved lettuce, as bedding elsewhere in the garden, not just because they look good and you can eat them, but because they're also a way of saying that the garden does not take itself too seriously and it's fun.

The circle of gravel is the hub of the garden and of the design. It's planted in a clever mixture of the formal – seven box balls equally spaced round the perimeter for structure in the winter – and the informal with two softer areas planted with herbaceous plants, like the small cream red-hot poker (*Kniphofia* 'Little Maid'), *Potentilla* 'Gibson's Scarlet', lady's mantle (*Alchemilla mollis*) and *Viola labradorica*, both of which will self-seed into the gravel, and Californian poppy (*Eschscholzia californica*) sown as seed into the soil around the other perennials before the gravel was raked back over. There are also several clumps of the tall golden oat grass (*Stipa gigantea*) to create a gauzy effect, like a veil in front of the long border. Dan sees the circle as a pool from which the rest of the garden draws its colours.

Louise and Learie continued to be utterly thrilled with the garden, and Louise is out there first thing every single morning, checking on progress overnight, seeing what's in flower or in bud or poking through the soil.

In less than two months after we'd planted it, the gravel circle already looked stunning, with the brilliant scarlet of the potentillas (*P.* 'Gibson's Scarlet'), the lime green of the lady's mantle (*Alchemilla mollis*), and the hot orange and yellow of the Californian poppies (*Eschscholzia californica*). By late August, you could get a very clear idea of how the garden will look when it's mature. Louise finds the plant associations just astounding and the questions all visitors ask her is how on earth did Dan Pearson know it was going to look so incredibly good when he came up with the plan? Louise just loves being in the garden and finds it all too easy to lose track of time completely. One Saturday lunchtime, she nipped out there for an hour or so's deadheading, went in, guiltily thinking it must be about half past three only to find it was nearly six o'clock.

TREES

Prunus pissardii 'Nigra' (sometimes sold as *Prunus cerasifera* 'Pissardii')
Its leaves open ruby red, then fade slowly to deep brownish purple. It also has pink flowers in late spring.
Approx. height and spread: 6 × 3m (20 × 10ft).

CLIMBERS

Clematis
C. 'Jackmanii', *C.* 'Etoile Violette' and *C.* 'Bill Mackenzie'. See page 96.

Ivy
Persian ivy (*Hedera colchica*)
This has large, oval-shaped, dark green leaves.
Approx. height and spread: 10 × 5m (30 × 15ft).

Irish ivy (*Hedera hibernica*)
The vigorous Irish ivy has large mid-green leaves and makes excellent ground cover under trees. See page 28.

Golden hop (*Humulus lupulus* 'Aureus')
Grown for its leaves, which start out butter-yellow and slowly fade to yellow-green, it is very vigorous but, if you cut it down each spring, you get lovely new foliage and keep it in check.
Approx. height and spread: 6 × 6m (20 × 20ft).

Jasmine (*Jasminum officinale*)
This vigorous scrambler has deliciously scented, small, white flowers from mid-summer to autumn. It responds well to cutting back to keep it in check.
Approx. height and spread (if left unpruned): 7.3 × 7.3m (24 × 24ft).

Japanese honeysuckle (*Lonicera japonica* 'Halliana')
Quick-growing and evergreen, this scented, white-and-yellow-flowered variety is ideal for covering walls and fences in sun or part-shade.
Approx. height and spread: 5 × 5m (16 × 16ft).

Chinese Virginia creeper (*Parthenocissus henryana*)
The leaves of this invaluable, shade-loving, self-clinging climber are a deep, velvety green with silvery veins – even more prominent when the foliage turns red in autumn.
Approx. height and spread: 10 × 10m (30 × 30ft).

Rosa 'Ena Harkness'

It has fragrant crimson-scarlet flowers all summer.

Approx. height and spread: 2.5 × 2.5 m (8 × 8 ft).

Chilean potato-vine *(Solanum crispum* 'Glasnevin')

This semi-evergreen scrambler has masses of purple-blue flowers with bright golden stamens from early summer to autumn. It's not 100 per cent hardy, so grow it against a south- or west-facing wall, and tie the new growth in.

Approx. height and spread: 6 × 3 m (20 × 10 ft).

SHRUBS

Japanese angelica tree *(Aralia elata)*

This architectural plant has very large, dramatic, olive-green leaves and panicles of white flowers borne on mature branches in late summer/early autumn.

Approx. height and spread after five years: 2 × 1.5 m (6 × 5 ft).

Butterfly bush *(Buddleia davidii* 'Black Knight')

This variety has the darkest violet-purple scented flowers from mid-summer to autumn and dark green leaves which are white underneath. See page 98.

Approx. height and spread after five years: 3 × 3 m (10 × 10 ft).

Box *(Buxus sempervirens)*

This small-leaved evergreen, ideal for topiary, will grow in sun or shade, on any soil.

Approx. height and spread after five years: 1 × 1 m (3 × 3 ft).

Dogwood *(Cornus alba* 'Aurea')

This variety, which has yellow-green foliage, does better in part-shade where the sun won't scorch its leaves. It also has red stems in winter and is best pruned back hard each spring for the best colour and to keep it small.

Approx. height and spread after five years (unclipped): 2.5 × 3 m (8 × 10 ft).

Pineapple broom *(Cytisus battandieri)*

This tall graceful shrub has silvery grey leaves and upright candles of yellow, pineapple-scented flowers in May and June. It's ideal trained on a sunny wall.

Approx. height and spread after five years: 3 × 2 m (10 × 6 ft).

Elaeagnus angustifolia 'Caspica' or 'Quicksilver'

A large shrub or small tree, it has slender silver leaves, bright in spring, darkening later and turning yellow in autumn, along with very fragrant, creamy yellow flowers in late

spring which may produce yellow fruits.
Approx. height and spread after five years: 3 × 2 m (10 × 6 ft).

Old English lavender (*Lavandula angustifolia*)
The tallest of the family, it has pale lavender-blue flowers and, some say, the best scent.
Approx. height and spread after five years: 1 × 1 m (3 × 3 ft).

Honeybush (*Melianthus major*)
This tender evergreen is grown for its huge, dramatic, blue-grey leaves made up of jagged oval leaflets.
Approx. height and spread after five years: 1 × 1 m (3 × 3 ft).

Jerusalem sage (*Phlomis fruticosa*)
Worth having for its wavy grey leaves, and its unusual, whorled, pale yellow flowers in early summer. Cut it back after flowering to keep it compact.
Approx. height and spread after five years: 1 × 1 m (3 × 3 ft).

Black bamboo (*Phyllostachys nigra*)
A dramatic feature plant with its startling blue-black canes and slender mid-green leaves.
Approx. height after five years: 6 m (18 ft); spread: indefinite.

Roses
R. glauca A graceful shrub with blue-grey foliage and small pink single flowers with a white centre which tone with the leaves. It has red-brown hips in winter.
Approx. height and spread: 2 × 1.5 m (6 ft 6 in × 5 ft).
R. 'Louis XIV', a China rose, produces deep crimson, almost black semi-double flowers more or less continuously through the summer with glossy but sparse foliage.
Height and spread: 60 × 60 cm (2 × 2 ft).

Sage (*Salvia officinalis* 'Purpurascens' group)
See page 101.

Cotton lavender (*Santolina pinnata neapolitana* 'Edward Bowles')
This version of the old favourite has feathery grey foliage and pale, creamy yellow flowers. It needs full sun and an open, free-draining soil.
Approx. height and spread after five years: 50 × 70 cm (18 × 28 in).

Spanish broom (*Spartium junceum*)
This almost leafless shrub is grown for its dark green stems and vivid yellow, fragrant pea-flowers in mid- to late summer.
Approx. height and spread after five years: 2 × 1 m (6 × 3 ft).

Laurustinus (*Viburnum tinus*)
This Victorian favourite has dark evergreen leaves and white flowers, pink in bud from late autumn to spring. It tolerates most soils and deep shade.
Approx. height and spread after five years: 1 × 1m (3 × 3ft).

PERENNIALS

Acanthus spinosus
See page 102.

Lady's mantle (*Alchemilla mollis*)
See page 102.

Angelica gigas
This member of the *Angelica* family, with lovely leaves and black stems, is not widely available, but you can find it in specialist nurseries.
Height and spread: 1 × 1m (3 × 3ft).

Coreopsis verticillata 'Moonbeam'
This has masses of pale yellow daisy flowers from June to September and finely divided, feathery leaves.
Height and spread: 40 × 30cm (16 × 12in).

Crocosmia 'Lucifer'
See page 103.

Epimedium × perralchicum
This attractive ground-cover plant for semi-shade has dark semi-evergreen rounded leaves and short spires of hanging yellow flowers on fine wiry stems. Cut off the old leaves in spring just before flowering.
Height and spread: 45 × 30cm (18 × 12in).

Euphorbia characias wulfenii
See page 103.

Euphorbia amygdaloïdes robbiae
Invaluable in dry shade, this has rosettes of dark green, leathery leaves and pale yellow bracts in spring.
Height: 45–60cm (18–24in); spread: indefinite.

Bronze fennel (*Foeniculum vulgare* 'Purpureum')
This striking aromatic herb is grown mainly for its feathery bronze leaves. Cut off the

Left: The vibrant yellows and oranges of the Californian poppies and the scarlet of the potentillas are seen through a haze of golden oats.

tiny, greeny yellow flowers which appear in July and August to prevent it seeding itself everywhere, and to get another flush of foliage.

Approx. height and spread: 2 m × 45 cm (6 ft × 18 in).

Bloody cranesbill *(Geranium sanguineum)*

This superb ground-cover plant produces spreading hummocks of deeply divided green leaves and saucer-shaped magenta flowers from June to September.

Height and spread: 25 × 30 cm (10 × 12 in) or more.

Hellebores

The stinking hellebore *(Helleborus foetidus)* has clumps of deeply divided, dark evergreen leaves and cup-shaped, pale green flowers in winter and early spring.

Height and spread: 60 × 45 cm (2 ft × 18 in).

The Lenten rose *(Helleborus orientalis)* has broader evergreen leaves and saucer-shaped flowers in very variable shades of white, yellow, purple and pink often freckled with crimson.

Height and spread: 45 × 45 cm (18 × 18 in).

Day lily *(Hemerocallis* 'Stafford')

This has dramatic, dark red flowers. See page 103.

Iris 'Deep Black'

This tall, bearded iris has deep velvet black and royal purple flowers late in the season.

Height and spread: 1.2 m × 30 cm (4 × 1 ft).

Red-hot poker *(Kniphofia* 'Little Maid')

This is a cooler, more delicate, version of the red-hot poker, with grassy leaves and spikes of cream flowers in summer.

Height and spread: 60 × 45 cm (2 ft × 18 in).

Plume poppy (*Macleaya cordata*)

This tall elegant plant has large, round, lobed, grey leaves, which are downy white underneath. The plumes of small pale flowers in summer are a bonus.

Height and spread: 1.5 m (5 ft) or more × 60 cm (2 ft) or more.

Miscanthus sacchariflorus

This vigorous perennial grass has smooth mid-green leaves that often turn bronze in the winter.

Height: 3 m (10 ft); spread: indefinite.

Bergamot (*Monarda* 'Cambridge Scarlet')

This has shaggy, bright red flowers on tall stems from mid-summer to early autumn.

Height and spread: 75 × 45 cm (2 ft 6 in × 18 in).

Solomon's seal (*Polygonatum × hybridum*)

A lovely, easily grown woodland plant, with elegant, arching stems and green-tipped white flowers hanging in pairs from the leaf stems.

Height and spread: 1 m × 40 cm (3 ft × 16 in).

Potentilla 'Gibson's Scarlet'

This has brilliant scarlet, saucer-shaped flowers from mid-summer on over dark green, strawberry-like leaves.

Height and spread: 45 × 45 cm (18 × 18 in).

Lungwort (*Pulmonaria saccharata*)

Larger than the ordinary lungwort, this has broader leaves strikingly spotted with silver. The flowers which appear in March–April open pink and change to blue.

Height and spread: 20–30 × 60 cm (8–12 in × 2 ft).

Coneflower (*Rudbeckia fulgida deamii*)

This has large, daisy-like, yellow flowers with central black cones in late summer and autumn.

Height and spread: 1 m × 60 cm (3 × 2 ft).

Golden oat grass (*Stipa gigantea*)

A lovely specimen grass, this forms dense clumps of grey-green grassy leaves which throw up elegant arching stems of tiny silvery flowers from June to September and persist into winter. The dead grass looks wonderful rimed with frost.

Height and spread: 2–2.5 × 1 m (6–8 × 3 ft).

Viola labradorica

See page 61.

· ANNUALS

Climbing gourds (*Cucurbita pepo*)
These half-hardy annual plants, grown like marrows or courgettes, can be trained up a trellis or bean poles.
Approx. height: 1–1.2 m (3–4 ft).

Cup-and-saucer vine (*Cobaea scandens*)
An evergreen, half-hardy climber grown in this country as an annual, it has yellow-green flowers that change to purple, freely borne from late summer to the first frosts, *provided* they have had enough sun early on.
Height: 4–5 m (12–15 ft).

Californian poppy (*Eschscholzia californica*)
A striking hardy annual with orange, yellow and sometimes cream flowers above finely cut blue-green foliage. It flowers best on poor sandy soil in full sun.
Height and spread: 30 × 15 cm (12 × 6 in).

Morning glory (*Ipomoea hederacea*)
A lovely annual climber with heart-shaped leaves, it has blue, pink, red or purple trumpet flowers from summer to early autumn.
Height: 3–4 m (10–13 ft).

Petunia
Very free-flowering half-hardy annual in a vast range of colours, being bred to be more weather-resistant all the time.
Height and spread: 25 × 30 cm (10 × 12 in).

Red oak-leaved lettuce (*Lactuca sativa*)
This has red-tinged leaves that can be pulled a few at a time.
Height and spread: 25 × 30 cm (10 × 12 in).

Ruby chard or seakale beet (*Beta vulgaris cicla* group)
A spinach-like plant with glowing ruby-red stems and midribs.
Height and spread: 60 × 30 cm (2 × 1 ft).

Runner bean (*Phaseolus coccineus*)
This gives you not only beans but scarlet, white or pink flowers and bright green heart-shaped leaves.
Height 3 m (10 ft).

THE LONG THIN GARDEN

*O*ne of the most common and most difficult types of garden to deal with from a design point of view – and that's true for back gardens and front gardens – is the long thin garden. You see them everywhere, belonging to houses in a whole range of different styles, from mid-Victorian to 1960s. All too often their owners have tried to make the garden seem as wide as possible by having only very narrow beds down the sides and a long narrow path, often right down the middle, both of which, in fact, have the opposite effect and only go to emphasize the narrowness of the garden.

Our long thin garden is attached to a pretty little semi-detached Victorian cottage but it has exactly the same problems as thousands of other front gardens. It belongs to teacher Bethan Clarke, who bought the house three years ago. It faces south and measures 15m (50ft) long × 6m (18ft) wide and, since at least half the width was taken up by the concrete drive, the garden area proper, then just laid to lawn, was only about 3m (10ft) wide. The fact that the drive and the lawn were two long thin strips side by side, leading straight to the house with nothing to break them up visually at all, only made the garden seem even longer and thinner than it actually was.

The garage was set back behind the house – one of a pair shared with the neighbours on the other side – so the drive was literally a means of getting from road to garage and wasn't used for parking. The boundary on the west-facing side was a low wall ending well before Bethan's drive merges into the shared drive up to the garages, with a bed on her side planted with some large conifers. The east-facing boundary between her house and the matching semi was a healthy yew hedge that needed little more than a trim and a feed. Between the garden and the road there was another hedge – elm, this time, regrown from a tree stump, and trimmed neatly – and a pair of wrought-iron gates left open all the time. The drive was flanked by two large junipers, which seemed to Bethan to stand like sentries, only emphasizing the boring rectangular nature of the garden.

When she bought the house there was a honeysuckle growing over the porch, and a herringbone cotoneaster along the wall under the front window to hide the electricity meter box. All she had added were a few perennials like columbine, primulas and some bulbs in front of the cotoneaster for spring colour.

Having spent most of her time getting the inside of the house as she wanted it, she was now ready to turn her attention to the front garden. What she hated most about it was the fact that it made the house look and feel so narrow, so she wanted a garden that would make it feel wider, more generous. The drive was a major problem, because it was so dominant, and she had wondered about the feasibility of moving it. She also wanted a garden she could enjoy from the window of the front room. As it was, she looked down a long, boring rectangle of lawn, beyond the hedge and straight on to a telegraph pole on the opposite corner with a tangle of wires radiating from it. Something to divert the eye from that would be welcome, too.

As the front garden faced south it was sunny for most of the day, and Bethan wanted to be able to sit in her garden in the summer after work, so a certain amount of privacy was important. But at the same time, she wanted to be able to watch the world go by – in other words, to see without necessarily being seen! The idea of water in the garden appealed to her, for movement – of water itself, and the constantly changing reflections of the sky – and to attract wildlife. While she wanted a garden where she could potter and learn about plants, her busy life meant she didn't have much time to devote to gardening, so a lowish-maintenance garden would be ideal. As for colours, she loves blue, but also likes soft peachy apricot shades – colours she had used in the living room.

We invited designer Jean Goldberry to tackle the problems of Bethan's garden, but at a distance – by post and by phone. Jean realized some time ago that for many people, particularly those who live in areas of the country where there aren't any local garden designers, it is just too expensive to get a design done for their garden in the conventional way. The time involved in a garden designer actually travelling to the site can make it prohibitively expensive.

So she has evolved a fool-proof method of working by post, which includes sending clients a comprehensive, easy-to-follow set of surveying instructions, explaining how to take precise measurements and work out levels, take a series of photographs to give her panoramic views to work from, indicate from a long list of possible features what they would like in the garden and even take several samples of soil from different parts of the garden which Jean then analyses back at her studio.

The design

Much of the skill in solving garden design problems lies in deceiving the eye – drawing it to where you want it to look and away from what you don't want it to see. In a long thin garden like Bethan's, your eye goes whizzing straight down the garden to the front of the house with nothing at all to divert it on the way, so the message that is sent very clearly to the brain is 'Long. Narrow. Boring'.

One very obvious way of tackling this problem is to break up the length by putting in strong lines going widthways which divert the eye, taking it across the garden and back again rather than straight up it, and creating the *illusion* of width. In the same way, on a much smaller scale, if you lay a path with the bricks going widthways, it will look much wider than a path of exactly the same dimensions with the bricks laid lengthways.

In this instance, Jean used curves to pull your eye across the garden and then back again. She took out the existing drive up as far as the house and put in a new drive which started on the other side of the garden and swept across in a gentle curve to join up with the communal one, leading to the garages beyond the house. To link the parking area with the front door, Jean put in a brick path which went past the door then swept round in a loop, cutting back across the centre of the drive to end in a small paved area with a seat, right up against the west-facing boundary, looking back up the garden to the house.

By making full use of the width of the garden and taking your eye backwards and forwards across it, Jean made it seem much wider than before. To combat the problem of 'desire lines' – the tendency of regular visitors to take the shortest route from A to B – Jean cleverly blocked off other routes in various ways and funnelled all traffic – motor and pedestrian – precisely where she intended it to go.

In any small garden, Jean is a great believer in going down and up, too, to increase the sense of space. To take the eye, and therefore the mind, downwards, she loves to use water and, since Bethan was keen to have a water feature, she created a tear-shaped pond almost 4m (13ft) long. Ever mindful of the potential dangers of a pool, though, she made it only a few inches deep, filled it with stones, and installed a powerful pump to create the effect of a stream burbling over them.

To take the eye up and out of the garden, she put in a simple, triangular pergola of rough-sawn timber to span the drive. There are three uprights close together near the west-facing boundary, and just two uprights, 2.5m (8ft) apart, on the other side of the drive. The crosspiece from the centre upright just rests on the piece of wood linking the two widely spaced uprights.

Much of Jean's work has been in very small gardens and she has often used mirrors, carefully angled to reflect particular areas of the garden and make the space seem literally

twice the size. She put two narrow mirrored panels – of perspex, not glass for safety reasons – in between the three uprights of the pergola to reflect the large planted container in front of them back and forth between them.

When she is designing any garden, Jean believes it is vital to create as many views as possible within the garden and to frame them. The pergola acts as a frame to three different views – first, the view of the house as you come into the drive, second of the feature with the mirrors and a planted container from the small seat outside the front door, and finally of the small seat and the front of the house, from the bench further down the garden.

Jean likes to use baskets, lined with plastic and painted with yacht varnish to make them waterproof, rather than terracotta or glazed pots because they are so much cheaper and you can afford to use really large ones for a strong impact. And Jean thinks it is very important to have big features – and big plants – in a small space. If you use only small ones there's a danger that the garden can wind up looking just too dinky. She placed one basket next to the small seat by the front door, and then two more in different sizes, going in a diagonal line down the garden.

As a barrier between the garden and the street, where the entrance to the old drive used to be, and running up the west-facing side of the garden, Jean has used attractive diamond trellis, and planned to cover it with climbing plants. It is much cheaper than a new brick wall, much quicker than a new hedge, and takes up less garden room, too.

Left: Without the evidence of the 'before' photograph (*left, above*), it would be hard to believe that this is a long thin garden. The sweep of the drive and the curved path cutting across it really do make it seem much wider than it is. The simple pergola (*above*) frames the front porch beautifully, while the dramatic variegated aralia in the basket draws your eye towards it.

To cope with the perennial problem of the dustbin, she designed a recessed store, just inside the entrance to the new drive, up against the fence and pushed as far back as possible into the one remaining juniper in the corner. It's made of the same green trellis and the climbers will grow over it as well, soon hiding the bin from view.

Building the garden

Jean's choice of hard materials in the garden was dictated by cost and the need for a natural feel. To edge the new drive and path, she used a double row of small concrete setts in soft shades of grey and plum. For the drive itself, on a well-compacted sub-base of hard core she chose pale brown chippings which are much larger and rougher than gravel and, once compacted, soon lock together to form a solid surface. For the path, she used brindle paviours laid on sand, except where it crossed the drive of course and would need to take the weight of a car. Here the paviours were set on the same solid sub-base as the rest of the drive. The garden slopes gently down towards the house, but using chippings for the drive rather than a solid material like concrete means that any excess water will simply soak through them and the hard core into the soil beneath, instead of causing a drainage problem near the house.

We made the pond, using a tough butyl liner, with a thick layer of builder's sand underneath to prevent any sharp stones in the soil making holes in it. The reservoir for the water, along with the outflow pipe, was housed in a brick-lined cavity under the drive with a recessed manhole cover, filled with chippings, on top. It meant access was very simple, but it also created an echo chamber, to amplify the sound of the water as it rushed out of the tank. The submersible pump was placed on a brick in a suitably deep hole, and covered with an inverted black plastic flower pot to filter out larger bits of debris. Since we were using a powerful pump, we chose not to use a low-voltage DIY system but got an electrician to do the wiring. Whichever system you opt for, though, it is vital to think about where the cable will go right at the start because the last thing you want is to put in your new hard landscaping and then realize that you've got to dig it up again to lay cable underneath. As we were laying our path, we put a piece of plastic tubing under the foundations, so that when the time came it was simple to feed the armoured cable for the pump and the lighting system through it.

We had planned to cover the plastic liner with large oval slate-grey pebbles (paddlestones) but they proved virtually impossible to get, since several local authorities have now forbidden quarrying for them on their beaches. Instead we used a few large boulders and slivers of slate. They have rough edges, of course, so we used off-cuts of pond liner underneath them to create a double layer and stop them puncturing the liner itself.

Lighting was an important practical as well as aesthetic consideration since the house is set well back from the road, so we installed lights with sensors to pick up the movement of cars or people on the drive and switch them on automatically. They are on timing switches, too, so that Bethan would have ample time to park her car and get indoors before they switched themselves off again.

The trellis we used for the boundary comes in a light green but, since we wanted to link it visually to the yew hedge on the other side of the garden, and the posts come in dark brown, we stained it all dark green. In fact the posts are a darker green than the panels because they started out darker, but it creates a very attractive effect. We used it again by the house and, since that section curves, we interspersed wide panels with narrow ones to make the curve, and for unity of design used the same combination of broad and narrow panels on the long straight section, too.

To support the climbers on the walls of the house we put up wires in a diamond pattern, using masonry nails with two small washers threaded on to them. The end of the wire is wrapped round and round between the two washers before the nail is finally banged home. It makes a more attractive pattern than the usual grid, but it also means that you get better coverage because the plants grow diagonally rather than straight up and across.

The soil test that Jean did on the samples Bethan sent her showed that it was slightly alkaline and rather poor, deficient in most nutrients except nitrogen. Before we planted anything, we gave the soil a really good feed with spent hops, which also helped it to retain moisture since it was very free-draining. To increase the fertility, we added a mixture of blood, fish and bone and dried seaweed for an instant boost, and bonemeal and hoof and horn for another boost, long term.

Planting

Having made three large new planting areas in the garden, Jean wanted to create different moods. In the south-west-facing corner of the garden, for instance, between the road and the back of the seat, she wanted a woodland feel with a few small trees to provide shade for shade-loving shrubs and perennials. The soil was too alkaline for acid-lovers like rhododendrons and pierises, but we planted two snowy mespilus (*Amelanchier canadensis*) as standard trees for their starry white flowers in spring and

The impact of what could have been a vast expanse
of drive is reduced by this attractive pattern made
with paviours, setts and chippings where path
crosses it.

vivid autumn colour. Underneath them, we planted woodland plants like *Eucryphia × nymansensis*, which eventually makes a large shrub, covered in large white flowers in late summer, *Euphorbia amygdaloïdes robbiae*, hellebores like a pink form of *H. orientalis* and the red-stemmed *H. foetidus* 'Wester Flisk', and hardy geraniums, like 'Ann Folkard', which has lime-green leaves and magenta flowers and loves to sprawl through other plants. We planted fuchsias like the red and purple 'Mrs Popple' and the softer pink 'Lena' and, along the sunnier, more open edge of the drive, we planted rosemary – the tall 'Miss Jessopp's Upright' – the more subtle geranium, *G. × cantabrigiense* 'Biokovo', which forms neat hummocks of fresh green leaves and has small blush-white flowers all summer, and spiky *Morina longifolia*, with rosettes of thistle-like evergreen leaves and tubes of small, pinky white flowers in summer; and among them all we planted drifts of feathery fennel (*Foeniculum*).

Under the remaining juniper in the south-east corner, we planted flame creeper (*Tropaeolum speciosum*), a vigorous relative of the nasturtium with flame-red flowers in summer, which looks wonderful climbing up dark conifers.

To scramble up the trellis by the entrance, Jean chose a stunning white passion flower (*Passiflora caerulea* 'Constance Elliott'), and she used it again to climb up one of the pergola posts, to give the illusion that it had already travelled a very long way. Behind the seat, we planted the purple-leaved vine (*Vitis vinifera* 'Purpurea') and, since she always has scented plants near seats, the highly fragrant virgin's bower (*Clematis flammula*) which carries masses of small white flowers in late summer and early autumn.

On the trellis curving round to the front door, there's the fragrant white jasmine (*Jasminum polyanthum*), golden hop (*Humulus lupulus* 'Aureus') and another scented clematis, the evergreen *C. armandii* which has white flowers in spring. On the trellis to the right of the front door is the scented passion flower *P.c.* 'Incense' and, to scramble up the front of the house itself, she opted for the Chilean potato-vine (*Solanum crispum* 'Glasnevin') and a white rose, 'Félicité Perpétue'.

For the area under the window Jean chose sun-lovers like the sun rose (*Cistus* 'Silver Pink') and the vivid blue-flowered *Ceratostigma plumbaginoïdes*, and, for winter scent, the evergreen *Daphne tangutica* with cottagey perennials like delphiniums, foxgloves (*Digitalis*) and campanulas planted in among them.

Around the margins of the pool there are dramatic foliage plants like the lush arum lily (*Zantedeschia aethiopica*), *Astilboides tabularis*, the fine feathery goat's beard (*Aruncus dioicus* 'Kneiffii') and the golden filipendula (*Filipendula ulmaria* 'Aurea'), and, for a splash of flower colour, blue irises and the white marsh marigold, *Caltha palustris* 'Alba'.

Along the east-facing border by the hedge, too, foliage is more important than flowers. By the two large boulders in the border, Jean chose a very delicate, thin-stemmed bamboo (*Himalayacalamus* – sometimes still called *Thamnocalamus* – *falconeri*) and illuminated it at night. There are ferns (*Dryopteris*), too, and grasses like the tufted hair grass (*Deschampsia flexuosa* 'Tatra Gold'). Against the dark green of the yew, gold foliage shows up really well, so there's also a spiky *Phormium* 'Yellow Wave' and, trained as a mop-headed standard, a variegated green and gold spindle (*Euonymus japonicus* 'Ovatus Aureus').

To disguise the telegraph pole, we made full use of perspective. To hide an eyesore beyond your boundary, the temptation is to plant something right *on* the boundary but, for it to do the job, it would have to be very tall indeed. Much better to site something

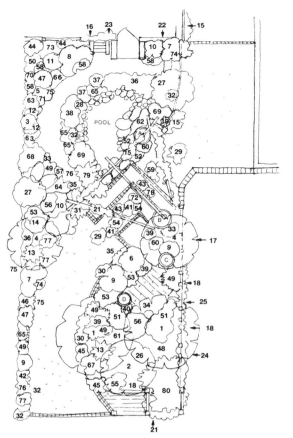

1 *Amelanchier canadensis*; 2 *Eucryphia nymansensis*; 3 *Euonymus* 'Ovatus Aureus'; 4 *Malus* 'Van Eseltine'; 5 *Ceratostigma plumbaginoïdes*; 6 *Choisya ternata* 'Sundance'; 7 *Cistus* 'Silver Pink'; 8 *Daphne tangutica*; 9 *Fuchsia* 'Mrs Popple'; 10 *Myrtus tarentina* 'Variegata'; 11 *Hebe* 'Caledonia'; 12 *Phormium* 'Yellow Wave'; 13 *Rosmarinus* 'Miss Jessopp's Upright'; 14 *Rosa* 'Blanche Double de Coubert'; 15 *Clematis armandii*; 16 *Clematis* 'Comtesse de Bouchaud'; 17 *Clematis flammula*; 18 *Clematis* 'Star of India'; 19 *Jasminum polyanthum*; 20 *Humulus lupulus* 'Aureus'; 21 *Passiflora* 'Constance Elliott'; 22 *Passiflora* 'Incense'; 23 *Solanum crispum* 'Glasnevin'; 24 *Tropaeolum speciosum*; 25 *Vitis vinifera* 'Purpurea'; 26 *Pleioblastus auricomus*; 27 *Himalayacalamus falconeri*; 28 *Deschampsia flexuosa* 'Tatra Gold'; 29 *Festuca glauca*; 30 *Milium effusum* 'Aureum'; 31 *Molinia caerulea* 'Variegata'; 32 *Dryopteris* 'Cristata The King'; 33 *Dryopteris erythrosora*; 34 *Acanthus spinosus*; 35 *Ajuga* 'Catlin's

Giant'; 36 *Anemone × hybrida* 'Honorine Jobert'; 37 *Aruncus dioicus* 'Kneiffii'; 38 *Caltha palustris* 'Alba'; 39 *Campanula latiloba*; 40 *Campanula ochroleuca*; 41 *Campanula cochleariifolia*; 42 *Corydalis flexuosa* 'Père David'; 43 *Cymbalaria muralis albiflora*; 44 *Delphinium* 'Guinevere'; 45 *Dianthus* 'Fair Folly'; 46 *Erodium reichardii*; 47 *Erysimum* 'Bowles' Mauve'; 48 *Euphorbia amygdaloïdes robbiae*; 49 *Foeniculum vulgare* (bronze); 50 *Foeniculum* (green); 51 *Filipendula rubra*; 52 *Filipendula ulmaria* 'Aurea'; 53 *Geranium pratense* 'Mrs Kendall Clark'; 54 *Geranium sanguineum*; 55 *Geranium × cantabrigiense* 'Biokovo'; 56 *Geranium* 'Ann Folkard'; 57 *Geranium wallichianum* 'Buxton's Variety'; 58 *Geranium robustum*; 59 *Geranium orientalitibeticum*; 60 *Helleborus foetidus* 'Wester Flisk'; 61 *Helleborus orientalis* pink form; 62 *Hemerocallis* 'Stella de Oro'; 63 *Hosta* 'Halcyon'; 64 *Hosta* 'Sum and Substance'; 65 *Iris sibirica*; 66 *Iris* 'Matinata'; 67 *Morina longifolia*; 68 *Penstemon heterophyllus*;

69 *Astilboides tabularis*; 70 *Salvia × sylvestris* 'May Night'; 71 *Schizostylis coccinea*; 72 *Thymus serpyllum* 'Goldstream'; 73 *Verbena bonariensis*; 74 *Viola cornuta*; 75 *Viola purpurea*; 76 *Viola cornuta* 'Alba'; 77 *Viola sororia* 'Freckles'; 78 *Wahlenbergia gloriosa*; 79 *Zantadeschia æthiopica*; 80 Existing juniper.

Baskets
A *Aralia elata* 'Variegata'; *Nicotiana alba* ('Domino'); Stock ('Legacy' – white); Dill; Fennel – green; Sage – golden; *Viola* 'Moonlight'; *Lobelia* (white); *Petunia* (white); *Bidens ferulifolia*.
B *Hydrangea macrophylla*; Dwarf french beans; *Hedera helix* 'Eva'; *Teucrium chamaedrys*; Sage – purple; *Lobelia* (blue and purple).
C *Salix caprea* 'Kilmarnock'; Stock ('Legacy' – purple); Parsley – French; *Viola tricolor* (purple); *Fuchsia* 'Lena'; *Lobelia* (purple and blue).
D *Hosta* 'Zounds'; Stock ('Legacy' – purple); Basil; Parsley; Chives; *Lobelia* (purple and blue).

**The long thin garden in
five years' time**

much smaller *closer* to the house between your usual vantage point and the eyesore. In order to arrive at the right spot, you need a helper, a long stick – a broom or rake handle will do nicely – a rag . . . and a thick skin. Get your helper to sit or stand in the usual vantage point – in Bethan's case, the living-room window – then tie the rag to the end of the broom, hold it up above your head with your arm stretched up as high as it will go and walk in a direct line towards the eyesore. Get your helper to yell when the rag is level with the top of the eyesore. If you then plant a tree which will grow to at least 4–4.5m (13–15ft) – roughly the height of your extended arm plus the length of the broomstick – on that very spot, you'll know that it will screen the eyesore. Any neighbours or passers-by who see you doing this will think you're barking mad – that's where the thick skin comes in – but it does the job very effectively.

Jean chose a narrow crab apple (*Malus* 'Van Eseltine') with lovely double pink flowers in spring, and both fruits and good colour. Under the hedge, we planted violas – the pretty, aptly named, blue 'Freckles' and the very pretty, recently introduced, blue corydalis *C. flexuosa* 'Père David'.

Since Jean chose to use large baskets in the design, they needed large bold planting, so we put a blue-flowered hydrangea (*H. macrophylla serrata*) with wall germander (*Teucrium chamaedrys*) spilling over the edges, in the biggest one in front of the mirrored panels, the Kilmarnock willow (*Salix caprea*) with some trailing fuchsias in another by the seat, a huge hosta in a third and the stunning variegated Japanese angelica tree (*Aralia*) with an assortment of herbs and bedding in the last.

As we had already put in lighting for security reasons, we added a few more lights to feature certain plants – the basket by the mirrors, for example, and the delicate bamboo beside the boulders.

We planted the garden in late April and by the end of the summer it was looking really lovely. The design was so skillful that the 'bones' in their own right were very striking, but a few months on, all the hard landscaping materials had mellowed in colour to very soft plums and greys while the planting had begun to soften it considerably. Really thorough soil preparation had paid dividends because all the plants were growing very well – the *Clematis flammula* had scrambled over large areas of trellis by the larger seat, the lovely white passion flower (*P.* 'Constance Elliott') had flowered for weeks and all the trailing hardy geraniums, like 'Ann Folkard' and *G. robustum* had done just that, covering large areas of ground. The containers were a huge success, overflowing with unusual combinations of plants, some of them, the dwarf beans and herbs, edible. Both the owner, Bethan Clarke and designer, Jean Goldberry who had masterminded the whole venture at arms' length by post and phone, were delighted with the way it had turned out.

TREES

Snowy mespilus (*Amelanchier canadensis*)
A superb tree for small gardens, it has white flowers in late spring, and light green leaves that turn brilliant orange-red in autumn when red berries also appear. It can be grown as a tree or as a multi-stemmed shrub.
Approx. height and spread after five years: 4.5 × 3 m (15 × 10 ft).

Eucryphia × nymansensis
This eventually makes a large shrub, carrying white saucer-shaped flowers in late summer over dark green leaves.
Approx. height and spread after five years: 2 × 1 m (6 × 3 ft).

Spindle (*Euonymus japonicus* 'Ovatus Aureus')
Less widely available than other spindle family members, this one has glossy, oval, evergreen leaves with creamy yellow margins. It's not quite as hardy as *E. fortunei*.
Approx. height and spread after five years: 1 × 1 m (3 × 3 ft).

Crab apple (*Malus* 'Van Eseltine')
This small slender tree has double pink flowers in late spring and rounded yellow crab apples in autumn.
Approx. height and spread after five years: 4 × 1.5 m (13 × 5 ft).

Kilmarnock willow (*Salix caprea* 'Kilmarnock')
If you must have a weeping willow in a small garden – or even in a pot – this is the one, with its purple-green stems and fat, silver-white catkins yellowing with age.
Eventual height and spread: 2–3 × 3 m (6–10 × 10 ft).

CLIMBERS

Clematis
C. armandii has long, oval, evergreen leaves and scented white flowers in early spring. Fast growing.
Height and spread: 6 × 6 m (20 × 20 ft).
C. 'Comtesse de Bouchaud' has large, soft, rose-pink flowers from July to August.
Height and spread: 2–3 × 1 m (6–10 × 3 ft).
C. flammula produces masses of small, single, scented, white flowers that smell of almonds in late summer and early autumn.
Height and spread: 3–5 × 2 m (10–15 × 6 ft).

C. 'Star of India' is very free-flowering with large, single, deep purple-blue flowers with a deep red stripe and brown anthers in mid-summer.
Height and spread: 3 × 1m (10 × 3ft).

Ivy (*Hedera helix* 'Eva')
This one has small grey-green leaves with cream variegation.
Approx. height and spread: 1.2 × 1m (4 × 3ft).

Golden hop (*Humulus lupulus* 'Aureus')
See page 33.

Jasmine (*Jasminum polyanthum*)
This tender, twining climber has pure white, highly scented flowers, pink in bud, in late spring and early summer.
Approx. height and spread: 5 × 5m (16 × 16ft).

Passion flower (*Passiflora*)
P. caerulea 'Constance Elliott' is a beautiful all-white cultivar of the familiar passion flower, flowering in summer and autumn.
Height and spread: to 10 × 10m (33 × 33ft).
P. 'Incense' has deep purple flowers and is also scented.
Height and spread: to 7 × 7m (23 × 23ft).

Chilean potato-vine (*Solanum crispum* 'Glasnevin')
See page 34.

Flame creeper (*Tropaeolum speciosum*)
This scrambler has six-lobed blue-green leaves and scarlet nasturtium flowers in summer followed by bright blue fruits. It's perfect for growing through a hedge, preferring its roots in shade and its head in sun.
Height and spread: 1.8 × 1.2m (6 × 4ft).

Purple-leaved vine (*Vitis vinifera* 'Purpurea')
Grown mainly for its purplish leaves that are covered in white down when young, it also has tiny greenish-white flowers and small purple 'grapes'.
Height and spread: 7 × 7m (23 × 23ft).

The mirrored perspex panels (*right*) are set at right
angles to reflect the basket planted with a blue
hydrangea, french beans and ivies back and forth
between them and create an attractive feature
from the house.

SHRUBS

Japanese angelica tree (*Aralia elata* 'Variegata')
This is a stunning architectural shrub for foliage effect, with creamy-white variegations on its huge leaves. It's more tender than the plain one and more expensive. See page 34.

Ceratostigma plumbaginoïdes
A very useful ground-cover plant, with bright blue flowers from July to November. Its leaves colour red in autumn.
Approx. height and spread: 45 × 20 cm (18 × 8 in).

Choisya ternata 'Sundance'
The golden form. See page 99.

Sun rose (*Cistus* 'Silver Pink')
This one has, not surprisingly, silver-pink flowers in long clusters, lasting only a day but produced in succession for weeks in summer. It also has attractive grey leaves.
Approx. height and spread: 60 × 75 cm (2 ft × 2 ft 6 in).

Daphne tangutica
This dwarf shrub has slender evergreen leaves and deliciously fragrant, white flowers tinged with purple in mid to late spring.
Approx. height and spread after five years: 10 × 30 cm (4 × 12 in).

Bamboo (*Himalayacalamus falconeri*)
An elegant bamboo with long yellow-green leaves on slender canes. It's not as hardy as some but, where it's happy, it can get extremely tall.
Approx. height and spread: 3–10 × 1 m (9–30 × 3 ft).

Fuchsia
'Mrs Popple' has typical fuchsia flowers in violet and crimson and roundish leaves with a purple tinge. The less hardy 'Lena' has double flowers in pale pink and magenta.
Approx. height and spread after five years: 1 × 1 m (3 × 3 ft).

Shrubby veronica (*Hebe* 'Caledonia' syn. 'E. B. Anderson')
This dwarf hebe has purple-flushed leaves and stems, and flowers that open deep purple and then fade, giving a two-tone effect. It needs a sunny sheltered spot.
Approx. height and spread after five years: 1 × 1 m (3 × 3 ft).

Lacecap hydrangea (*Hydrangea macrophylla serrata*)
See page 118.

Myrtle (*Myrtus communis tarentina* 'Microphylla Variegata')
This tender variety has small, narrow, aromatic leaves margined with white and small white tufted flowers in summer, followed by white berries.
Approx. height and spread after five years: 1 × 1 m (3 × 3 ft).

Phormium 'Yellow Wave'
An elegant evergreen foliage plant, this one has long, narrow, upright leaves, golden with green edges. Older plants produce clusters of small bronze-red flowers in mid-summer.
Approx. height and spread after five years: 60 × 60 cm (2 × 2 ft).

Pleioblastus auricomus
See page 104.

Rosmarinus 'Miss Jessopp's Upright' See page 119.

Roses

Rosa rugosa 'Blanche Double de Coubert' is a lovely rugosa rose with strongly scented, pure white, almost fully double flowers all summer long. Its rough-textured light green leaves turn yellow in autumn.
Approx. height and spread: 1.5 × 1.2m (5 × 4ft).
Rosa 'Félicité Perpétue'. See page 74.

Wall germander (*Teucrium × lucidrys* or *T. chamaedrys*)
With its little steel-grey leaves and small lilac-pink flowers from July to September, it's a useful dwarf hedging plant.
Approx. height and spread: 20 × 50cm (8 × 20in).

PERENNIALS

Acanthus spinosus
See page 102.

Astilboides tabularis (syn. *Rodgersia tabularis*)
In moist soil and a sheltered spot, its scalloped, almost circular, light green leaves can reach 1m (3ft) in diameter. Creamy white flowers are borne well above the plant.
Approx. height and spread: 1 × 1m (3 × 3ft).

Bugle (*Ajuga reptans*)
A valuable ground-cover evergreen with spikes of blue flowers in spring. See also page 21.
Approx. height and spread: 10 × 30cm (4 × 12in).

Japanese anemone (*Anemone × hybrida* 'Honorine Jobert')
See page 102.

Goat's beard (*Aruncus dioicus* 'Kneiffii')
This is the most beautiful form, with finely divided leaves and plumes of minute cream flowers in summer. It needs a moist soil.
Height and spread: 1m × 45cm (3ft × 18in).

Marsh marigold (*Caltha palustris*)
Another moisture-loving plant, *C. p.* 'Alba' has white flowers for months in summer, and handsome rounded leaves.
Height and spread: 30 × 45cm (12 × 18in).

Campanula
The tall *C. latiloba* carries stiff stems of cup-shaped lavender-blue flowers in summer

above green rosettes of leaves.

Approx. height and spread: 1 m × 45 cm (3 ft × 18 in).

The rare *C. ochroleuca* has creamy bell-flowers in mid to late summer.

Approx. height and spread: 45 × 30 cm (18 × 12 in).

Fairy thimbles (*C. cochleariifolia*) makes spreading mats of tiny round leaves with small typical campanula blue flowers in summer.

Height: 8 cm (3 in); spread: indefinite.

Corydalis flexuosa 'Père David'

The fashionable plant of recent years, this has sky-blue spurred flowers with a tinge of purple over leaves like the maidenhair fern's.

Approx. height and spread: 30 × 30 cm (12 × 12 in).

Ivy-leaved toadflax *(Cymbalaria muralis albiflora)*

A plant that grows wild on walls, it has tiny, ivy-shaped, pale green leaves and tubular white flowers.

Approx. height and spread: 5 × 12 cm (2 × 5 in).

Delphinium (Guinevere group)

This has spikes of flowers in mixed shades of pale blue.

Approx. height and spread: 1.2 m × 30 cm (4 × 1 ft).

Tufted hair grass *(Deschampsia flexuosa* 'Tatra Gold')

An evergreen, tuft-forming, golden grass with plumes of flowers that last well into winter.

Approx. height and spread: 1 m × 30 cm (3 × 1 ft).

Modern pink *(Dianthus* 'Fair Folly')

This long-flowering pink has single flowers varying from dusky pink to dusky purple with two white splashes on each petal.

Approx. height and spread: 30 × 23 cm (12 × 9 in).

Foxglove *(Digitalis purpurea* 'Alba')

This is the lovely white form of the common foxglove.

Approx. height and spread: 1–1.5 m × 60 cm (3–5 × 2 ft).

Fern *(Dryopteris)*

Japanese shield fern (*D. erythrosora*) has divided fronds, coppery-pink when young and fading to a golden green, which last until mid-winter.

Approx. height and spread: 45–60 × 45 cm (18 in–2 ft × 18 in).

Erodium reichardii

Like a miniature hardy geranium, this makes a mound of tiny oak-like leaves with

saucer-shaped pink flowers with darker veins all summer.
Height and spread: 7.5 × 6 cm (3 × 2½ in).

Erysimum 'Bowles' Mauve'
See page 120.

Euphorbia amygdaloïdes robbiae
See page 36.

Filipendula
Meadowsweet (*F. palmata* 'Rubra') has large jagged leaves and feathery plumes of bright pink flowers on tall stems in mid-summer.
Approx. height and spread: 2–2.5 × 1.2 m (6–8 × 4 ft).
Golden filipendula (*F. ulmaria* 'Aurea') has divided bright golden-yellow leaves in spring, which turn pale green in summer and creamy flowers in clusters in mid-summer. Both filipendulas need a moist soil and part-shade.
Approx. height and spread: 30 × 30 cm (12 × 12 in).

Fennel (*Foeniculum vulgare*)
See page 36.

Cranesbill (*Geranium*)
G. 'Ann Folkard' has deeply cut, yellowish-green leaves and, in summer and autumn, masses of bright magenta flowers with black veins.
Approx. height and spread: 50 cm × 1 m (20 in × 3 ft).
G. × *cantabrigiense* 'Biokovo' has small blush-white flowers.
Approx. height and spread: 25 × 30 cm (10 in × 1 ft).
G. orientalitibeticum has cup-shaped pink flowers with white centres in summer, with leaves that are deeply cut and marbled in different shades of green.
Height in flower: 15–25 cm (6–10 in); spread: indefinite.
G. pratense 'Mrs Kendall Clark', like other meadow cranesbills, has handsome, deeply divided leaves which colour in autumn and pale blue, double flowers in early summer.
Height and spread: 60 × 60 cm (2 × 2 ft).
G. robustum is a tall, sprawling plant with blue-green leaves and lilac-pink flowers all summer.
Approx. height and spread: 75 × 30 cm (30 × 12 in).
G. sanguineum has deeply divided, dark green leaves and deep magenta flowers blooming profusely for many weeks.
Approx. height and spread: 30 × 45 cm (12 × 18 in).
G. wallichianum 'Buxton's Variety' has a non-stop display of blue flowers with white

centres from mid-summer to autumn; It's good for growing through other plants.
Approx. height and spread: 30 × 50 cm (12 × 20 in).

Hellebores

H. foetidus 'Wester Flisk' is a red-stemmed form of hellebore, with deeply divided, dark green leaves and clusters of hanging, cup-shaped, green flowers in late winter and early spring.
Approx. height and spread: 45 × 45 cm (18 × 18 in).

The flowers of *H. orientalis*, which vary from palest greeny-white to a deep plum that's almost black, are carried in late winter and early spring.
Approx. height and spread: 40 × 60 cm (18 in × 2 ft).

Hemerocallis 'Stella de Oro'

See page 103.

Hostas

H. 'Halcyon' has heart-shaped grey-blue leaves in shade, with heavy clusters of violet-mauve flowers in mid-summer.
Approx. height and spread: 30 cm × 1 m (1 × 3 ft).

H. 'Sum and Substance' (also sometimes sold as 'Sun and Substance') has huge, thick-textured, golden leaves, with pale lavender flowers in July. It is more slug-resistant than many.
Approx. height and spread: 45 cm × 1 m (18 in × 3 ft).

Iris

I. 'Matinata' is a dark purple-blue bearded iris which flowers in early summer.
Height: 1 m (3 ft); spread: indefinite.

The Siberian flag (*I. sibirica*) has smaller flowers in veined blue or blue-purple from late spring to early summer and much narrower leaves. It likes moist soil.
Approx. height: 50 cm–1.2 m (20 in–4 ft); spread: indefinite.

Bowles' golden grass (*Milium effusum* 'Aureum')

A lovely grass for a shady spot, with bright yellow leaves, stems and flowers.
Approx. height (of flowers) and spread: 60 × 30 cm (2 × 1 ft).

Purple moor grass (*Molinia caerulea* 'Variegata')

It forms dense clumps of short, soft leaves striped with cream, and plumes of tiny buff flowers.
Approx. height (of flowers) and spread: 60 × 30 cm (2 × 1 ft).

Morina longifolia

A curious plant with rosettes of thistle-like evergreen leaves and a long stem of tubular

flowers, starting white and turning pink in summer.
Approx. height and spread: 1 m × 30 cm (3 × 1 ft).

Penstemon heterophyllus
Narrow, pale green leaves and funnel-shaped, pure blue flowers for a long period in summer.
Height and spread: 25 × 25 cm (10 × 10 in).

Salvia × *sylvestris* 'Mainacht' or 'May Night'
See page 105.

Kaffir lily (*Schizostylis coccinea*)
This has grass-like leaves and crimson flowers on slender spikes in September and October. It likes moist soil and full sun.
Approx. height and spread: 60 × 23 cm (2 ft × 9 in).

Creeping thyme (*Thymus serpyllum* 'Goldstream')
The leaves of this very low-growing form are green splashed with gold.
Approx. height and spread: 2.5 × 60 cm (1 in × 2 ft).

Verbena bonariensis
Tall, angular, branched stems bear heads of fragrant lavender-blue flowers from June onwards above rosettes of rough green leaves.
Approx. height and spread: 1.5 m × 60 cm (5 × 2 ft).

Violas
V. cornuta: see page 121. *V. c.* 'Alba' is the lovely white form of the horned violet. *V. c.* 'Purpurea' group (also called *V. labradorica*) is very vigorous and seeds itself everywhere but makes a very useful and attractive ground cover. *V.* 'Moonlight' is creamy yellow and *V. sororia* 'Freckles' has flowers of palest blue flecked with violet in April and May.
Approx. height and spread: 10–15 × 15 cm (4–6 × 6 in).

Wahlenbergia gloriosa
An unusual plant for sun or part-shade, it has large, starry, deep blue to purple flowers on wiry stems in summer above shiny mats of foliage.
Approx. height and spread: 15 × 15 cm (6 × 6 in).

Arum lily (*Zantedeschia aethiopica*)
A striking architectural plant for a pool-side, it has large, spear-shaped, glossy, green leaves and the familiar white arum flowers. It needs moist soil and, since it's not hardy everywhere, it will benefit from winter protection.
Approx. height and spread: 1.2 m × 60 cm (4 × 2 ft).

THE SLOPING GARDEN

*A*lthough we had tackled a sloping garden in the first series of *Front Gardens*, we had, to be honest, tackled the easier option. A garden that slopes down from the house to the street is less problematic than one that slopes down from the street to the house. So we decided to put that right. There is no doubt that gardens sloping this way are challenging both technically and in terms of design, and our sloping garden was a real challenge.

The house was a small semi, built in the 1930s on an acute-angled corner, with the garden sloping down to the house in two directions. The front gate was right at the apex, and there was a purely functional path of four slabby concrete steps – all different lengths – leading from the gate to the front door. It was quite dangerous at night because the garden was very dark. There were boundary hedges on either side of the front gate – a mixture of green and golden privet and laurel – which were very thin in parts and in need of cutting back hard and feeding. There was another hedge – of the dreaded leylandii this time – between the semis, which belonged to the neighbours. It was 5m (16ft) tall, with parts of it either badly hacked or dead.

The house is home to Emily and Gary Leister and their three sons – Scott, five, Jack, four, and one-year-old baby Max. In 1990, they started building an extension at the side of the house where the garage used to be. Gary and his father did most of the work themselves when they could fit it in – mainly at weekends and in the holidays – so it took four years and, during that time, the front garden became little more than a site for storing building materials and a tip for all the rubbish – the subsoil dug out from the foundations, broken breeze-blocks and so on. In fact it looked so daunting that the advice that sprang most readily to mind was, 'Move!'

The garden had once been quite pretty, but that was so long ago that Emily couldn't really remember what it was like and she was desperate to turn it into a garden once again. She loves plants and so wanted the front garden to be her haven, somewhere to potter once the children were in bed. There's a back garden, mainly lawn, where the boys can play, so the front garden could justifiably be her domain.

The new extension finishes only about 2m (6ft) from the hedge at the side of the garden, so the bank from the road to the base of the extension's side wall was now very steep indeed, and Gary had already built part of a retaining wall of breeze-blocks to hold it back. They had also planned an area of hardstanding at the top for the car, so that was something else to be borne in mind in the design – steps down from the parking area, for instance, and a way of screening it as far as possible from the rest of the garden.

The pluses were that the garden was a good size, an interesting shape, well screened from the road, and it faced south-south-west. It wasn't possible to say what the soil was until all the subsoil was cleared and we had reached top soil underneath, but it was likely to be rather gravelly and alkaline since that was typical of the area.

The design

New Zealand-born designer Christopher Masson – no faint heart he – wasn't daunted by our sloping garden at all. On the contrary, he was very excited by the prospect since he finds gardens on different levels much more interesting visually than those on the flat. A garden that slopes down towards the house, he pointed out, is laid out for you to see as you look out of the window, offering the possibility of cascades of colourful plants.

One of Emily's early thoughts about the front garden had been to remove the path altogether, since it chopped the garden so comprehensively into two, and put the new entrance at the side by the new extension with a flight of steps coming down to the front door. Chris felt that would be something of a lost opportunity since it would mean scuttling down to the house rather than taking a more leisurely stroll through the garden, getting maximum enjoyment from it on the way and really feeling, when you did reach the front door, that you had arrived somewhere attractive to be.

Emily also wanted a lawn – even a little patch of lawn – to sit on in the summer evenings as the top left-hand corner of the garden caught the last of the evening sun.

Since the front of the house is the back-drop to every front garden, Chris wanted to link the two and make them complement each other. He liked the natural wood window frames on the extension, but wasn't so keen on the modern glazed front door. Nor were Emily and Gary. In fact they were planning to replace it anyway since one of the boys had fallen some time earlier and hit the lower panel with his head. Fortunately he wasn't hurt, but the glass was cracked right across. Something more in keeping with the style of the house – a traditional solid wood door – seemed a better bet. The same was true of the front gate – wrought-iron didn't look right either and since Chris wanted to make more of the entrance anyway, that was ripe for replacement too.

One of the major problems with a garden that slopes steeply down to the front door is that it can seem to tower over the house, making it feel dark and oppressive. Obviously, the garden would have to be terraced in some way, creating level areas backed by retaining walls, and Chris's solution was to push the slope, as far as possible, away from the house and up to the hedge by the front gate and on the right-hand side of the garden. So instead of turning the slope into several terraces of equal size, he designed a flight of four quite steep steps close together leading down from the broader, more substantial new landing, just inside the front gate, to a large flat area in the middle of the garden, creating a sense of spaciousness and airiness.

Much of this area would be a rectangular lawn, about 4 × 3m (13 × 10ft), with paving slabs set in the grass in a broad, irregular band across it, to the right of centre, continuing the line from the steps to the front door. This provided a dry, serviceable path but, at the same time, no longer chopped the garden into two visually, as the old concrete path had done, because what your eye registered primarily was the sweep of green grass across the entire width, not the path.

It was also a very practical idea, as was the brick edge around the lawn, because it meant that you could mow right across the whole area with no fiddly, time-consuming edging to be done. In the top left-hand corner of the lawn, which catches the last of the evening sun, Chris had used more stepping stones to form an area large enough to take a couple of chairs. And in two of the other corners, he'd used a few more stepping stones to balance it, and to stop the lawn appearing too neat and angular.

Moving on towards the front door, the band of stepping stones, set in concrete now, became two more steps between raised beds. The doorstep was already about 23cm (9in) above the ground, so Chris carried on the new path straight to it, leaving a narrow air gap between it and the house so as not to breach the damp-proof course.

To make the beds on either side of the path, Chris put in low brick walls 23cm (9in) high and about 60cm (2ft) from the house, creating a useful sunken service path of coarse gravel around the base of the walls.

On the east-facing side of the garden Chris built two low terraces for planting and put in a path from the front door and steps up to the car parking area. By pushing the slope to the edge of the garden, he had made the bank up to the hedge even steeper, a bit like a cliff face. That gave him the idea for using large pieces of Westmorland rock, laid either side of the steps, which would look very natural – as if the soil had been washed away down the slope, exposing the rock beneath. To separate the garden from the hard-standing, he put in some trellis, an arch and a gate.

The other main materials in the garden were frost-proof bricks to match the house walls, and imitation York stone slabs.

To add interest to the rather flat front of the house, Chris added a simple porch, and trellis across the new extension and the other side of the house to link it all together.

Building the garden

Clearing the garden of four years' worth of debris was the first step. To have carted it all out by wheelbarrow up that steep slope would have taken days, and both morale and backs would probably have given out long before it was finished. So we hired a Mini-veyor, an electrically operated conveyor belt, which comes in sections and can be put together to the required length so that you can just pile rubbish on to it and watch it travel straight out into a waiting skip.

When it comes to building a garden that slopes down to the house, the major problems are to do with drainage. If you just leave it as a slope, a heavy downpour will leave you with several centimetres of water slopping around the base of the house walls and, despite functioning damp-proof courses, if that happens too often the bottom of the wall and the foundations may become damp. A really heavy downpour will bring soil down as well, which not only leaves you ankle-deep in mud, but also leaves the roots of any plants exposed and liable to damage.

The obvious solution to the slope itself is terracing. It's essential that any retaining walls, whether they're made from brick, stone or wood, are really solid and on good deep footings because they are holding the soil back and, if they collapse, you'll have your garden on the front doorstep. It's a job for a professional bricklayer, or someone with a great deal of DIY experience. Gary and his father, for example, having built the extension, could have done the job themselves, given time, but we needed the building work finished quickly to give the plants the longest possible growing season. Once the walls were built and the mortar was dry, we painted them on the inside with a special waterproof membrane to stop the moisture from the soil seeping into the bricks. But the weight of wet soil behind even a well-built retaining wall could be enough to push it down, so there must be 'weepholes' in the first course of bricks in the wall – made either by just leaving a half-brick gap, or mortaring in short lengths of clay drainage pipe every metre or so. A cheaper alternative is plastic piping, but white is rather garish so it's best painted a dark colour.

In most instances there were beds below our retaining walls, so the soil would soak up almost all the excess water since it is dry and free-draining anyway. By the house,

Levelling the centre of the sloping garden and terracing the rest has made it appear much bigger, while the new porch and front door, much more in keeping with the style of the house, have transformed that too.

though, what little water there was from the very low retaining walls could drain through the gravel and along an existing gully to a drain.

The pieces of rock, carefully chosen so that they could be man-handled into place by two strong men and a wheelbarrow, were part-buried in the soil for stability.

The porch was built of rough-sawn timber and tiled with cedar shingles. Although they are a reddish colour when they're new, they soon fade to a silvery grey, so we stained the other timber, which wouldn't fade, the same silvery shade so that it would eventually all blend in to together. The new trellis was stained the same colour.

Since one of the main colours in the planting scheme was to be blue, we decided to match the paint for the new door and front gate to a blue flower. Most paint shops now have these magic machines which can blend seven hundred or more different shades, and the local paint shop was able to match the rich purply blue of the *Ceanothus* exactly. Painting front door and front gate the same colour is a very good and simple way of linking house and garden, especially when they are in line with each other.

The hedge by the front gate was scooped down on either side – we used spray paint to mark out the curve – to make the entrance more imposing. Since the hedge was looking a bit scrappy in parts, we pruned it hard back, cleared all the weeds from the base, gave it a good feed of Growmore to get the new growth going and made sure it was well watered.

Although Chris had been tempted to remove the leylandii hedge – with the owner's permission – he decided that, unattractive as it was, it provided a useful windbreak and helped filter out noise from the street. So we got a tree surgeon to reduce it in height and cut out the dead wood. There had been a fence on Gary and Emily's side of the hedge, but the roots had pushed it over and it had rotted away. We therefore put in a new fence, 2m (6ft) high, partly to screen some of the gaps in the hedge and partly as insurance in case the new owners next door – it was on the market – wanted to chop the conifers down. We stained it dark brown to make it less prominent.

To illuminate the steps, and to extend Emily's evening pottering time, we put in a low-voltage, DIY lighting system. The final step was a simple micro-irrigation system with very small plastic pipes coming off a main hose, with either sprinklers or drip-nozzles attached, also DIY, permanently attached to an outside tap.

Planting

The aspect – sunny for most of the day – and the soil, which turned out to be free-draining, thin and just on the limy side of neutral, were the first factors in Chris's choice of plants. In fact there is a huge range of plants, many Mediterranean, others from

California and southern Africa, which really thrive in these conditions.

As for the colours, since Emily liked most shades, the choice was largely dictated by the colour of the house bricks, and so Chris chose pale yellows, white, strong blue, with a few touches of red – orange-red rather than blue-red – and rich purple.

The soil on that west-facing side of the garden was particularly thin and dry, since the leylandii sucked out nutrients and moisture, so Chris decided to make a virtue of necessity and chose plants that revel in those conditions: shrubs like the Californian lilac (*Ceanothus papillosus roweanus*), with its tough, deep green, leathery, evergreen leaves and beautiful thimbles of purple-blue flowers in early summer, a variegated snowberry (*Symphoricarpos*) that Chris planned to clip into balls, and holly-leaf sweetspire (*Itea ilicifolia*), an arching evergreen with tassels of white flowers in late summer. Trained against the fence itself, there were the climbing hydrangea (*H. anomala petiolaris*), the white solanum (*S. jasminoïdes* 'Album') and the sweet-smelling star jasmine (*Trachelospermum jasminoïdes*). Either side of the steps by the front gate, Chris wanted to emphasize the entrance with a pair of standard clipped privets and, beneath them, in the corners, we planted an unusual euonymus (*E. fortunei* 'Minimus'), a rounded, low-growing, spreading shrub with tiny green leaves, which would spill over the wall and soften the sharp angles.

In the bed to the east of the steps, the plants were chosen largely for their foliage: a small mop-headed hawthorn (*Crataegus persimilis* 'Prunifolia') grown primarily for its autumn colour and to provide shade for the shade-loving plants around it, the silver variegated holly *Ilex aquifolium* 'Silver Milkboy' and the short, stubby-leaved bamboo, *Shibataea kumasasa*, the hosta 'Royal Standard' and, for some flower colour, the vivid blue variegated lesser periwinkle (*Vinca minor* 'Alba Variegata') to trail over the walls, along with one of the loveliest osteospermums, 'Silver Sparkler'.

On the other side of the steps were the spiky-looking plants – yucca, phormium, libertias and irises, and, in the corner, a weeping tree, *Cercidiphyllum japonicum* 'Pendulum'. Although it colours best in autumn in an acid soil, it will normally cope with some alkalinity. Here, though, it did not thrive so we replaced it in late summer with a plain green Japanese maple (*Acer palmatum*).

In the lower of the two sunny east-facing beds, Chris chose shrubs like *Daphne* × *burkwoodii* and some with silvery foliage like Russian sage (*Perovskia atriplicifolia*) with almost white stems and soft blue flowers, and *Convolvulus cneorum*. There were pinks, too, like *Dianthus* 'Cranmere Pool' and the trailing *Convolvulus sabatius* with intense blue trumpets, with the cranesbill (*Geranium wallichianum* 'Buxton's Variety') to scramble through all its neighbours. In the centre was a large deep blue Chinese bell pot, simply planted with the silvery and finely divided dusty miller (*Senecio cineraria* 'Ramparts') and the pale 'Cambridge Blue' lobelia.

In the bed above, there was rosemary (*Rosmarinus officinalis*) and a swathe of lavender –

1 *Lonicera* × *americana*; 2 *Libertia formosa*; 3 *Iris foetidissima*; 4 *Phormium tenax*; 5 *Euphorbia longifolia*; 6 *Acer palmatum*; 7 *Lavandula* 'Munstead'; 8 *Rosmarinus officinalis*; 9 *Yucca filamentosa*; 10 *Melianthus major*; 11 *Genista aetnensis*; 12 *Thymus vulgaris*; 13 *Geranium wallichianum* 'Buxton's Variety'; 14 *Phygelius capensis*; 15 *Erigeron karvinskianus*; 16 *Teucrium fruticans*; 17 Welsh poppies; 18 *Convolvulus sabatius*; 20 *Rosa* 'Kent'; 21 *Sedum* 'Autumn Joy'; 22 *Allium schoenoprasum*; 23 *Clematis viticella*; 24 *Acaena caesiiglauca*; 25 Standard *Rosa* 'Graham Thomas'; 26 *Lamium* 'White Nancy'; 27 *Laurus nobilis*; 28 *Clematis montana* 'Alba'; 29 ferns in crevices; 30 *Campanula portenschlagiana*; 31 Pinks in crevices; 32 *Wisteria sinensis* 'Alba'; 33 *Trachelospermum jasminoïdes*; 34 *Abutilon megapotamicum*; 35 *Iris* 'Jane Phillips'; 36 *Cotoneaster horizontalis*; 37 *Sisyrinchium*; 38 *Fuchsia*, *Bidens* and *Lobelia* 'Cambridge Blue' in pot; 39 **Annuals various**; 40 *Epilobium glabellum*; 41 *Pittosporum tenuifolium*; 42 *Solanum jasminoïdes* 'Album'; 43 *Nandina domestica*; 44 *Itea ilicifolia*; 45 *Hydrangea petiolaris*; 46 *Ceanothus roweanus*; 47 *Symphoricarpos orbiculatus* 'Variegatus'; 48 *Cyclamen hederifolium*; 49 *Liriope muscari*; 50 *Euonymus fortunei* 'Minimus'; 51 *Vinca minor* 'Alba Variegata'; 52 *Hosta* 'Royal Standard'; 53 *Shibataea kumasasa*; 54 2 standard *Ligustrum*; 55 *Helleborus argutifolius*; 56 *Ilex* 'Silver Milkboy'; 57 *Crataegus prunifolia*; 58 *Phyllostachys nigra*; 59 *Dryopteris filix-mas* 'Linearis'; 60 *Senecio cineraria* 'Ramparts'; 61 *Thymus vulgaris*; 62 *Hebe* 'Margret'; 63 *Rosa* 'Félicité Perpétue'; *Rosa* 'Schoolgirl'.

The sloping garden in
five years' time

the small *Lavandula angustifolia* 'Munstead' variety. At the back, to be trained on as bare stem to tumble over the rocks, there was a Mount Etna broom (*Genista aetnensis*) with bright yellow scented pea-flowers in spring. In among the rocks, Chris chose alpines like acaena, sea pink (*Armeria*) and a dark red sedum (*S. telephium maximum* 'Munstead Dark Red') and an unusual low-growing shrub, *Muehlenbeckia complexa*, which has small, round, evergreen leaves on very wiry stems which creep over rocks and twine happily through other plants. Where we planted alpines vertically in between two rocks, we wrapped their rootballs in pieces of dead turf first. The roots of the grass hold the soil together and the dead grass itself provides water-retentive organic matter to get the plant off to a good start. At the corner, at the bottom of the steps, we planted a standard rose, the yellow 'Graham Thomas'.

In the bed by the door there were roses, the pure white ground-cover rose 'Kent', and shrubby veronica (*Hebe* 'Margret'), which has blue flowers in mid-summer fading slowly to palest blue and then white, so you get a two-tone effect.

To climb up and over the porch, Chris chose the rose 'Schoolgirl', with orange-apricot flowers that fade to salmon-pink – just the thing to gee up the soft, subtle blue and white planting around it. On the other side of the path, also to climb up the porch, is 'Félicité Perpétue', a rambler with fragrant blush-white pom-pom flowers. To climb up the house walls on both sides of the front door, Chris opted for white wisteria. On the left he also planted the tender perennial climber, *Rhodochiton atrosanguineum*, with its drooping blood-red flowers, and on the right-hand side the wall shrub *Abutilon megapotamicum*, too, with its curious hanging red and yellow flowers in late summer.

The large bed under the window was to be filled primarily with seasonal planting, with another even larger blue Chinese bell pot in the centre. That was planted with *Fuchsia* 'Thalia', with its slender, hanging, burnt orange flowers and large deep green leaves, pale blue lobelia and bidens, the lovely trailing plant with yellow daisy flowers and feathery foliage.

Before we put it in place, at the end of May when all danger of frost had passed, we marked out the bed (sand in an empty wine bottle is a good way of doing it) into large drifts in which to sow annuals. Within the informal shapes of the drifts, it's best to sow the seed in straight drills because at least that way you know, when they've germinated, which are seedlings and which are weedlings.

Around the pot itself, we sowed feathery white cosmos and nasturtiums (*Tropaeolum majus*) – a single-coloured variety called 'Peach Melba' to take over at the end of the summer – along with drifts of rich blue cornflowers (*Centaurea*), baby blue-eyes (*Nemophila insignis*) and the poached-egg flower (*Limnanthes douglasii*). We also planted some more bidens around the pot to link the whole scheme together.

Four months later, it was hard to believe this was the rubbish tip we had started out with in early spring. The garden felt much bigger for one thing and seemed to belong much more to the house, what with the new porch and trellis work allowing climbing plants like wisteria and roses to unite the two. Apart from the problem we'd had with the Katsura tree (*Cercidophyllum japonica* 'Pendulum'), all the other plants established themselves well and started growing away. The lovely white ground cover rose 'Kent' was a great success, flowering profusely right through the summer.

In the spaces we'd had to leave between the permanent planting, we'd used annuals – good old busy lizzies, lobelia to soften the hard edges of the terracing walls, and deep blue salvias. Half-hardy perennials like the yellow daisy-flowered bidens, the soft yellow osteospermum 'Buttermilk', as well as the milk-white 'Silver Sparkler' with variegated foliage also added welcome colour. In June, Emily had discovered that she was expecting another baby just after Christmas, and hadn't been able to be quite as active in the garden as she'd intended. However, it was relatively easy to look after and a real pleasure to sit in in the evenings, just as she wanted it to be.

CLIMBERS

Clematis
C. montana 'Alba' is very vigorous, with masses of white flowers in May.
Approx. height and spread: 7–12 m (22–40 ft).
C. viticella is a late-flowering clematis with nodding purple-mauve flowers.
Approx. height and spread: 2–3 m (6–10 ft).

Climbing hydrangea (*Hydrangea anomala petiolaris*)
See page 116.

Lonicera × *americana* or × *italica*
See page 97.

Cape leadwort (*Plumbago auriculata*)
This fast-growing evergreen climber, with trusses of delicious sky-blue flowers from summer to early winter, needs a very warm sheltered spot outside – or grow it in a greenhouse.
Approx. height and spread: 3–6 × 3–6 m (10–20 × 10–20 ft).

Rhodochiton atrosanguineum
A tender evergreen climber which is usually grown as an annual here, with deep maroon bell-like flowers from late spring to late autumn. It needs a very sheltered warm spot or, again, grow it in a greenhouse.
Approx. height and spread: 3 × 3 m (10 × 10 ft).

Roses

R. 'Félicité Perpétue is a vigorous climber with clusters of small, creamy white, double, rosette-shaped flowers with a touch of pink from mid-June to the end of July.

Approx. height and spread: 4.5 × 3 m (15 × 10 ft).

R. 'Schoolgirl' is a modern climber with highly scented, coppery-orange flowers. Its foliage is rather sparse, though, so it's a good one to grow with other climbers.

Approx. height and spread: 3 × 2.5 m (10 × 8 ft).

Solanum jasminoïdes 'Album'

A semi-evergreen twiner for a warm sheltered wall or fence, it has star-shaped, scented, white, potato-flowers with yellow centres in summer–autumn.

Approx. height and spread: 4 × 4 m (13 × 13 ft).

Star jasmine *(Trachelospermum jasminoïdes)*

This evergreen climber with highly scented white flowers in summer and long oval leaves also needs a very warm sheltered spot outside or the protection of a greenhouse or conservatory.

Approx. height and spread: 3 × 3 m (10 × 10 ft).

Wisteria sinensis 'Alba'

Its fresh green leaves are well worth having after the strongly scented pea-like flowers carried in loose clusters in early summer are over.

Approx. height and spread: 8.4 × 8.4 m (28 × 28 ft).

SHRUBS AND TREES

Abelia × *grandiflora* 'Francis Mason'

This late-flowering shrub has golden variegated leaves, and pale pink, hanging, bell-shaped flowers in small clusters.

Approx. height and spread after five years: 1 × 1 m (3 × 3 ft).

Abutilon megapotamicum

A shrub for a sunny wall, with hanging, bell-shaped, red and yellow flowers borne from late summer to early autumn.

Approx. height and spread after five years: 1.5 × 1.5 m (5 × 5 ft).

Japanese maple *(Acer palmatum dissectum* Viride group)

This cut-leaved Japanese maple, which has lovely autumn colour, will tolerate slightly limey soil provided it gets enough moisture.

Approx. height and spread after five years: 80 cm × 1 m (2 ft 6 in × 3 ft).

Californian lilac (*Ceanothus papillosus roweanus*)
This variety has small, narrow, evergreen leaves and dense clusters of purple-blue flowers in late spring/early summer on arching branches.
Approx. height and spread after five years: 2.5–3 × 2.5–3m (7–10 × 7–10ft).

Cercidiphyllum japonicum 'Pendulum'
The weeping version of this small tree, grown primarily for its superb autumn colour.
Approx. height and spread after five years: 5 × 3m (16 × 10ft).

Convolvulus cneorum
This has silvery, silky leaves all year and white trumpet flowers, pink in bud, from late spring to mid-summer.
Approx. height and spread after five years: 45 × 60cm (18in × 2ft).

Herringbone cotoneaster (*Cotoneaster horizontalis*)
The branches form a herringbone pattern on a bank or against a wall. It has single white flowers in late spring, and red berries in autumn. Its leaves become bright red before they fall.
Approx. height and spread after five years: 60cm × 1m (2 × 3ft).

Hawthorn (*Crataegus persimilis* 'Prunifolia')
Clusters of white flowers in early summer are followed by red berries in autumn. Its attractive, glossy, dark green leaves colour well in autumn.
Approx. height and spread after five years: 2.5 × 1.5m (8 × 5ft).

Burkwood's daphne (*Daphne × burkwoodii*)
This deciduous daphne has clusters of sweetly scented pale pink flowers from late spring to early summer.
Approx. height and spread after five years: 60 × 45cm (2ft × 18in).

Euonymus fortunei 'Minimus'
A prostrate form of the familiar euonymus, with tiny, soft, plain green leaves.
Approx. height and spread: 10 × 60cm (4in × 2ft).

Fuchsia 'Thalia'
This stunning shrub isn't hardy but is worth treating as an annual.
Approx. height and spread: 1 × 1m (3 × 3ft).

Mount Etna broom (*Genista aetnensis*)
It has sea-green stems, barely any leaves, and masses of bright golden pea-flowers in early summer. Grow it as a large shrub or small bare-stemmed weeping tree but, as it hates being pruned, leave enough space.
Approx. height and spread after five years: 2.5 × 2.5m (8 × 8ft).

Shrubby veronica (*Hebe*)

H. 'Autumn Glory' has deep purple-blue flowers in short spikes and purple-tinged leaves from early summer to late autumn.

Approx. height and spread after five years: 30 × 75 cm (12 × 30 in).

The compact *H*. 'Margret' has sky-blue flowers that fade to white in late May or early June, followed by further flushes in late summer and autumn.

Approx. height and spread: 30–40 × 45–60 cm (12–15 in × 18 in–2 ft).

Holly (*Ilex aquifolium* 'Silver Milkboy')

Typical spiny leaves of this smaller-than-average variety have attractive, central, creamy white variegations. It's male, so has no berries.

Approx. height and spread after five years: 1.5 × 1.2 m (5 × 4 ft).

Holly-leaf sweetspire (*Itea ilicifolia*)

This spectacular but slightly tender shrub has 40 cm- (15 in)-long tassels of scented greenish-white flowers in late summer and holly-like evergreen leaves.

Approx. height and spread after five years: 1 × 1 m (3 × 3 ft).

Bay (*Laurus nobilis*)

The versatile bay can be kept in a container, clipped or left to grow freely, though it needs a sheltered spot since cold winds can scorch the leaves.

Approx. height and spread after five years: 1.5 × 1 m (5 × 3 ft).

Lavender (*Lavandula angustifolia* 'Munstead')

See page 118.

Honeybush (*Melianthus major*)

See page 35.

Muehlenbeckia complexa

This unusual twining climber or ground-cover plant has small dark green leaves on slender wiry stems. Tiny, star-shaped, white flowers in mid-summer are followed by waxy white berries.

Approx. height and spread: 60 cm × 1 m (2 × 3 ft).

Sacred bamboo (*Nandina domestica*)

See page 100.

Russian sage (*Perovskia atriplicifolia*)

Lavender-blue flowers in late summer are carried on almost white stems. The silver leaves are aromatic and may turn yellow in autumn.

Approx. height and spread: 75 cm × 1 m (2 ft 6 in × 3 ft).

New Zealand flax (*Phormium tenax*)
See page 56.

Cape figwort (*Phygelius capensis*)
This has yellow or orange tubular flowers from late summer through to early autumn. Grow it in a warm sheltered spot as a shrub or against a wall where it will reach up to 2 m (6 ft).
Approx. height and spread after five years: 1 × 1 m (3 × 3 ft).

Pittosporum tenuifolium
Flower arrangers love its slightly twisted, grey-green leaves on black twigs. In mild areas, small chocolate-brown flowers may appear in late spring on mature shrubs.
Approx. height and spread after five years: 1.5 × 1 m (5 × 3 ft).

Roses
R. 'Graham Thomas', grown here as a standard on a 1.2 m (4 ft) stem, is a new English rose with rich, yellow, scented flowers.
   R. 'Kent' is a modern ground-cover rose, with large trusses of pure white flowers.
Height and spread: 1.2 × 1.2 m (4 × 4 ft).

Rosemary (*Rosmarinus officinalis*)
It has narrow, aromatic, grey-green leaves and pale blue flowers in spring. Cut it back regularly to keep it bushy.
Approx. height and spread after five years: 75 cm × 1 m (2 ft 6 in × 3 ft).

Dusty miller (*Senecio cineraria* 'Ramparts')
Along with very white, felted, finely cut leaves, it has yellow daisies in summer but, if you cut off the buds, you get another flush of foliage instead.
Approx. height and spread: 30 × 30 cm (1 × 1 ft).

Snowberry (*Symphoricarpos orbiculatus* 'Foliis Variegatis')
This one has grey-green leaves with yellow margins, and tiny pink flowers in spring, but rarely fruits.
Approx. height and spread after five years: 1 m × 60 cm (3 × 2 ft).

Variegated woodsage (*Teucrium scorodonia* 'Crispum Marginatum')
The young leaves have the strongest variegations. It also has cream flowers in mid-summer.
Approx. height and spread: 30 × 30 cm (1 × 1 ft).

Lesser periwinkle (*Vinca minor* 'Alba Variegata')
The variegated version of this useful plant. See page 105.

Adam's needle (*Yucca filamentosa*)
The edges of the sword-like, upright leaves are covered with small white threads. Mature plants have creamy white flowers on upright spikes 1–2m (3–6ft) high in mid/late summer.
Approx. height and spread after five years: 1 × 1m (3 × 3ft).

PERENNIALS

Acaena
This family forms mats of attractive leaves and seedheads or burrs that last until winter. *A. buchananii* has grey-blue leaves and round green flowerheads in summer that develop into yellow-green burrs.
Approx. height and spread: 2.5 × 75cm (1 × 30in).
A. caesiiglauca is taller and more vigorous, with waxy blue leaves and brownish red burrs.
Approx. height and spread: 5 × 75cm (2 × 30in).

Chives (*Allium schoenoprasum*)
An invaluable herb, but also a good decorative plant with tall grassy leaves and round mauve flowers in early summer.
Approx. height and spread: 12–25 × 5–10cm (5–10 × 2–4in).

Sea pink, thrift (*Armeria maritima* 'Alba')
This forms mats of narrow, dark green, grassy leaves with small white flowers in summer.
Approx. height and spread: 10 × 15cm (4 × 6in).

Bidens ferulifolia
This trailing tender plant with ferny leaves and small, bright yellow daisy flowers is excellent for containers.
Approx. height and spread: 20 × 60cm (8in × 2ft).

Campanula portenschlagiana
See page 120.

Chasmanthium latifolium
A bright green grass with locket-shaped flowerheads.
Approx. height: 70 × 60cm (2ft 3in × 2ft).

Convolvulus sabatius
A trailing plant with intense blue-purple, trumpet-shaped flowers in summer and early autumn, it is good over walls and in baskets or tubs.
Approx. height and spread: 15–20 × 30cm (6–8 × 12in).

Cyclamen hederifolium
This autumn-flowering bulb has small pale pink flowers just before, or at the same time as, attractive ivy-shaped leaves, marbled with silver.
Approx. height and spread: 10 × 15cm (4 × 6in).

Deschampsia flexuosa 'Tatra Gold'
See page 58.

Dianthus 'Cranmere Pool'
This pink has double white flowers with a crimson base to each petal.
Approx. height and spread: 25 × 25cm (10 × 10in).

Fern (Dryopteris)
D. filix-mas 'Linearis' is a tall delicate variety of the male fern.
Approx. height and spread: 1.2 × 1m (4 × 3ft).
The Japanese shield fern (D. erythrosora): see page 58.

Epilobium glabellum
This makes useful ground cover with cup-shaped white flowers on slender stems in summer.
Approx. height and spread: 20 × 15cm (8 × 6in).

Fleabane (Erigeron karvinskianus or mucronatus)
Masses of small daisies that open white, then fade to pink and red from mid-summer on.
Approx. height and spread: 10–15cm × 4–6in; spread: indefinite.

Euphorbia longifolia
Grown for its fine foliage with pink edges to the white-veined leaves, it has the usual showy green-yellow flowers in spring.
Approx. height and spread: 60 × 60cm (2 × 2ft).

Pink strawberry (Fragaria 'Pink Panda')
This has bright pink strawberry flowers from late May till November and semi-evergreen leaves and occasionally produces fruit.
Approx. height: 10–15 × 20cm (4–6 × 8in).

Cranesbill (Geranium)
G. wallichianum 'Buxton's Variety': see page 59.
G. × cantabrigiense has masses of rounded leaves covered by soft mauve-pink flowers in summer.
Approx. height and spread: 23 × 30cm (9 × 12in).

Rock rose (*Helianthemum* 'Wisley White')
See page 103.

Hosta 'Royal Standard'
This one has heart-shaped, slightly puckered, rich green leaves and scented white flowers.
Approx. height and spread: 90 × 60 cm (3 × 2 ft).

Iris
Gladwin or stinking iris (*I. foetidissima*) is grown for its handsome dark green leaves and large vivid orange-red seedheads all winter.
Approx. height and spread: 45 × 60 cm (18 in × 2 ft).
I. 'Jane Phillips' is a pale blue tall bearded iris.
Approx. height: 1 m (3 ft).

Dead-nettle (*Lamium maculatum* 'White Nancy')
This is lovely silver ground cover for shade, with white flowers.
Approx. height and spread: 15 × 45 cm (6 × 18 in).

Libertia formosa
A good spiky plant for a sunny spot, with green leaves, sprays of white saucer-shaped flowers in early summer, and orange seedpods in autumn.
Approx. height and spread: 90 × 60 cm (3 × 2 ft).

Liriope muscari
Invaluable for dry shade, this has spikes of tiny bright violet flowers in autumn and evergreen grass-like leaves.
Approx. height and spread: 30 × 45 cm (12 × 18 in).

Welsh poppy (*Meconopsis cambrica*)
An invaluable gap-filler, this has ferny, fresh green leaves and vivid, lemon-yellow poppy flowers. It seeds itself prolifically.
Approx. height and spread: 45 × 30 cm (18 × 12 in).

Osteospermum 'Silver Sparkler'
This tender perennial has large white daisy flowers with a pearly blue sheen to the backs of the petals and a vivid peacock-blue eye. 'Buttermilk' has lovely soft yellow petals.
Approx. height and spread: 30–60 × 30–60 cm (1–2 × 1–2 ft).

Sedum telephium maximum 'Munstead Dark Red'
Good for sprawling over rocks, this has fleshy, dark green, purple-flushed leaves and flat flowerheads of dusky brown-red.
Approx. height and spread: 45 × 30 cm (18 × 12 in).

Bamboo (*Shibataea kumasasa*)
A slow-spreading Japanese bamboo, it has broad, dark green leaves.
Approx. height and spread: 1–1.5m × 30cm (3–5 × 1ft).

Sisyrinchium striatum
This has iris-like leaves and narrow spikes of pale yellow flowers.
Approx. height and spread: 30 × 23cm (12 × 9in). Flower stems: 60cm (2ft).

ANNUALS

Cornflower (*Centaurea cyanus*)
The best blue variety is 'Blue Diadem', while among the dwarf varieties 'Baby Blue' is good.
Height and spread: 30–75 × 15–30cm (1ft–2ft 6in × 6in–1ft).

Gypsophila elegans
This annual variety has clouds of tiny white flowers from mid-summer to early autumn.
Height and spread: 60 × 30cm (2 × 1ft).

Poached-egg plant (*Limnanthes douglasii*)
This ground-covering annual has yellow and white flowers for months and ferny, bright green foliage.
Height and spread: 15 × 10cm (6 × 4in).

Lobelia erinus **'Cambridge Blue'**
It has trailing stems of pale blue flowers all summer long.
Approx. height and spread: 10–20 × 10–15cm (4–8 × 4–6in).

Sweet alyssum (*Lobularia maritima*)
The familiar annual with tiny rounded heads of scented white flowers in summer and early autumn.
Approx. height and spread: 7.5–15 × 20–30cm (3–6 × 8–12in).

Baby blue-eyes (*Nemophila insignis*)
This fast-growing, bushy annual has bowl-shaped flowers with a white eye all summer.
Height and spread: 20 × 15cm (8 × 6in).

Nasturtium (*Tropaeolum majus*)
This invaluable annual with flowers in a range of colours from pale apricot to deep mahogany does best in poor, dry soil.
Height and spread: 30cm × 30cm–2m (1 × 1–6ft).

FOUR IN A ROW – MODERN TOWN HOUSES

*T*here's no doubt that the gardens people remember most vividly from the first series of *Front Gardens* were the four in the Victorian terrace. Perhaps it was the fact that they were so small, and that the houses themselves were very attractive and, of course, as they faced on to a footpath and not a street they didn't have to cope with the bane of 20th-century living – the car!

This time round, we decided to make life really difficult for ourselves, and took on another four in a row – four three-storey town houses, built in 1972.

The fronts were rather stark and anonymous – like the workhouse, one of the owners said – dominated by the integral garage doors, and with no obvious way of knowing which front door belonged to which house. Indeed, after I'd been chatting to an owner one day, he turned to go indoors and wound up trying to open the wrong front door!

The gardens were very small – only 4.2 × 6m (14 × 20ft) – with almost half the width taken up by concrete driveways, leaving a patch of garden proper scarcely bigger than those in the Victorian terrace.

Even so, in practical terms, the drives weren't wide enough. When cars parked on them, passengers had to step out on to next door's garden. And once a car was parked on the drive, the only pedestrian access to the front door was across the grass – not ideal in winter when it was wet and muddy. Since there were no boundaries between the houses – and couldn't be since people wouldn't be able to open their car doors – tradesmen just took the shortest route from door to door, so anything planted en route had to be either very low-growing or very tough to survive.

There were keen gardeners in all four houses, as the equally small but well-tended and interesting back gardens amply testified. They face due south which is a big advantage, while the fronts face north and are often exposed to a bitingly cold wind.

Each family had tried to do something with their front gardens – a tree here, a few shrubs there – but they had all more or less given up and settled for a small patch of lawn. Just to make their joy complete, slap bang in the centre of each patch of green was an inspection cover! They'd all tried to disguise them by sticking containers on top, but all that did was draw attention to the eyesore even more.

They all wanted to make their front garden more attractive. Carol Pope at No 21 wanted lots of colourful flowers from flowering shrubs, though a garden that looked good in winter was also important. The Gibbses at No 22 were keen to get rid of the lawn and, since they didn't have much time for gardening, to replace it with easy-to-care-for plants that looked good all year round. At No 23 the Fosters wanted some unusual and challenging plants, while the Amblers at No 24 wanted a design with imagination – which they felt was sorely lacking in the original garden – full of colourful plants, some of them fragrant to welcome them home in the evenings and something to make passers-by stop and admire.

The design

These are not the sort of gardens that you would normally associate with designer Jane Fearnley-Whittingstall, whose romantic Gertrude Jekyll garden won a gold medal at Chelsea in 1993, but she relished the challenge. While they were four individual gardens, they were also identical spaces and so shared the same problems. Jane's first thought was that all these gardens and the houses were a testament to our love-affair with the car since by far the most dominant features were the driveways and the garage doors, especially as three of them were painted colours which leapt out at you – bright blue, pillar-box red and white respectively.

Uppermost in her mind as she tackled the design was how to make the drives far less dominant but, at the same time, ensuring they could still function as access to the garages and as hardstanding. By treating the whole space in front of each house as one, instead of treating drive and garden as two separate elements, she gave herself much more room for manoeuvre.

The rather stark lines of the houses didn't worry her as she saw immediately the potential for softening them with plants – climbers like the ivy the Amblers had already trained up their wall – and, since the owners all got on so well, she saw it as an opportunity for some of the more vigorous climbers to grow across several houses.

She also saw the potential of large window-boxes on the ledge above the garages, with plants trailing down – preferably a range of different ivies blending in with the different foliage colours in each garden. Since the garage doors swung up to open, they would simply brush any trailing growth aside without damaging it. It would be impractical to climb up ladders with watering cans, so Jane suggested installing an automatic irrigation system, controlled from just one house for ease of maintenance.

Since there were no doorsteps, just a rather steep and abrupt step up from the path to the porch, she created a new broad step for each house, each one a slightly different shape. To solve the unavoidable problem of passengers having to step out on to next door's garden, Jane planned an area of hard landscaping carefully sited in the relevant place each time. The only way to ensure they were right was actually to see for herself where the cars usually parked and where the passengers usually stepped out.

Although we were dealing with four individual gardens, they ran in to each other, so Jane felt she should carry some sort of theme through them all, while at the same time giving each one a very clear identity.

To link the gardens, she repeated various materials in the hard landscaping. Imitation York slabs, gravel and brick, for example, are used in different patterns and combinations in Nos 21 and 22, while Nos 23 and 24 have the same timber edgings, and No 24 has the same slabs as the first two gardens.

No 21

In Carol Pope's garden, slabs in different shapes – squares and oblongs – were laid in interlocking rectangles, with an edging of brick breaking up the larger areas. While there were some gaps in the paving to accommodate plants, most of the planting was concentrated in two main areas – to the left of the drive, on the extra bit of land that garden has since it is on the corner, and to the right, where the lawn used to be.

No 22

In Phil and Karen Gibbs's garden, Jane used slabs in just one size, the small square ones, edged with brick, while the same bricks, laid in a herringbone pattern, were used to make the path, which starts out as half of the drive then curves round and straightens up again as it reaches the new front step. The rest of the drive consists of brick-edged slabs, some brick-edged areas of gravel and others left for planting, cleverly worked out so that the car's wheels don't actually go over the plants.

No. 23

Jane had planned to use gravel again, this time as the main hard material in the Japanese-style garden she had created for Pam Foster. But then Pam revealed she disliked gravel because it was messy, got trodden into the house, and passing children liked to chuck it around. So it was back to the drawing board on that one! After various experiments, we reached a compromise, with a very thin layer of gravel rolled into a layer of a much finer gravel which is rolled wet to bind it together. The net result on the drive

Left and below: Thanks to the new designs and planting of the gardens, these four modern town houses have lost much of their former bleakness while the new colours for the garage doors also add to a much softer overall look.

Right: Just one of four different permutations of brick, slabs and gravel used in the hard landscaping.

area was the *look* of gravel which is perfect for a Japanese-style garden which Pam liked, with few of the practical drawbacks. In the drive area, for a bit of fun, Jane had created informal planting areas in the shape of a map of Japan. The other Japanese elements in the garden were careful groupings of large rocks, with moss from Jane's greenhouse gutter transplanted into the hollows, a 'river' made from large smooth grey pebbles and really chunky wooden edgings in Tannalized timber specially treated to prevent rot.

No 24
In Pauline and Tony Ambler's garden, Jane used the same stone slabs in a variety of sizes this time, laid in a random pattern, with plenty of space for planting, while timber edgings provided a contrast in texture and a visual link to No 23.

Building the gardens

Clearing the gardens was very straightforward, breaking up the hated concrete runways, and getting rid of the grass. Some of the owners wanted to save a few plants, so we dug those up carefully, taking a good ball of soil round the roots. Those we wanted to use were put into pots and kept well watered and the rest were found new homes. We got a qualified tree surgeon to take out the tree in No 23 because it was very close to the house and needed a professional's skills to avoid any damage.

Although all four of Jane's designs made the drives part of the gardens, the areas that cars would drive over were given proper foundations of hardcore and compacted roadstone, strong enough to take the weight, even though the paving materials on top were the same as those laid on a bed of sand or wet-and-dry mix elsewhere in the gardens for lighter pedestrian traffic. We used good-quality imitation York stone slabs, which are cheaper than the real thing, and frost-proof bricks. If you want to use bricks in the garden, make sure they are frost-proof: ordinary house bricks aren't, and they will flake if the frost gets at them. We used seconds, which are cheaper than top-quality and have only a cosmetic flaw – the colour of a particular batch might not be right, for example – not a structural one.

To solve the problem of the inspection covers, we replaced the old metal ones with special recessed covers designed to hold hard materials – slabs, bricks or gravel – or soil so that they blend in with the surrounding area and all you see is a thin metal line around the edge. They're just as easily removed when necessary and every bit as strong as the old ones, so pose no problem in terms of safety. We also planted low-growing shrubs around them – conifers, cotoneaster, laurel – so that their branches would grow across the covers, but could be easily pushed aside for access to the drain.

We disguised the garage doors, too, by painting them softer, more reticent colours like mossy green and pearl grey to tone in with the foliage colour in each garden. Jane didn't think that painting them all the same colour would help, since each house needed every bit of individuality it could get to distinguish it from its neighbours. But as Jane puts it, 'Now, instead of saying, "Ours is the one with the bright red garage door," they can say, "Ours is the one with the subtle sludgy green door"!'

Planting

The main challenge here was that the gardens face north and are rather exposed, which reduces the choice of plants considerably. While Jane chose a large number of tough shade-lovers, she also felt encouraged by the supposedly tender hebe in Pauline's garden which flowered so early each year and by the fact that the pavement end of the gardens did get a fair bit of sun in summer, and so she was inclined to take a few chances with plants that, in theory, wouldn't be tough enough.

With the colour schemes, Jane went for a definite theme for each garden but, at the same time, blended it with the garden next door.

No 21

Jane was keen to use silvery foliage here since, with the extra bit on the corner, it was the only garden sunny enough for it to do well. So she used *Brachyglottis* 'Sunshine' (*Senecio*, as was), lavender, catmint (*Nepeta*), lamb's lugs (*Stachys byzantina*) and sage (*Salvia officinalis*). She kept the flower colours to white – Mexican orange blossom (*Choisya ternata*), Japanese anemones ('Honorine Jobert'); pale yellow – *Potentilla fruticosa* 'Primrose Beauty' and day lilies (*Hemerocallis* 'Golden Orchid'); and blue – lavender, catmint and sage; with splashes of orange in the potentilla 'Sunset' and the bright bracts of *Euphorbia griffithii* 'Fireglow' and the red-orange *Crocosmia* 'Lucifer' to liven it up.

Each garden was to have its feature plant, and in this garden it was an apple tree, *Malus domestica* 'Discovery', grown on a dwarfing rootstock, M 106, to keep it small. In the planting gaps on the drive, Jane also used silver foliage plants – low-growing rock roses (*Helianthemum*), dead-nettle (*Lamium maculatum*), and the blue grass *Festuca glauca*. We discovered later that because the family car is fitted with a catalytic converter, there was a very slight risk that the heat from the engine could set the grass on fire, so we replaced it with very low-growing thyme (*Thymus* 'Pink Chintz' and the gold variegated (*T.* 'Doone Valley'), and used the grasses to fill in the odd gap in the planting elsewhere in Carol's garden.

Jane used some of the same plants on the other side of the drive as well to link the two parts of the garden – brachyglottis, lavender, white Japanese anemones, potentilla 'Sunset' and another small apple tree, the finest of the russets, 'Egremont Russet'. The two apples will pollinate each other.

There was a core of evergreens for winter interest, too, like the blue horizontal juniper, 'Hughes', to help disguise the inspection cover. Since the local cats almost killed the catmint at the junction of the drive and the pavement, we moved it back and replaced it with a much less cat-attracting plant – another prostrate juniper – *J. squamata* 'Blue Carpet'. For the house walls, Jane chose a range of climbers, from a late-flowering clematis, *C.* 'Bill Mackenzie', the fragrant pale pink climbing rose 'Kathleen Harrop' and an ivy – the cut-leaved *Hedera helix* 'Green Ripple' – to climb up the wall to the right of the front door.

For the troughs in this garden, she chose the ivy 'Green Ripple' to link up with one growing up the house, and the lovely silvery grey-green and cream 'Glacier' to pick up the silver foliage in the rest of the garden.

No 22

In Karen's and Phil's garden the foliage was primarily plain green, ranging from the fresh apple-green of *Hebe rakaiensis*, to the deeper blue-green of the tall spurge, *Euphorbia wulfenii*. The main flower colours were soft peaches and apricots – the perpetual rose 'Buff Beauty', the potentilla 'Daydawn' and a lovely day lily (*Hemerocallis* 'George Cunningham') – with some white, too, most spectacularly in the lacecap viburnum (*V. plicatum* 'Mariesii'), which is the feature shrub in this garden. It was planted in front of the inspection cover and its low, tiered branches would eventually disguise it beautifully. As an accent, Jane included the odd splash of blue and purple like the spreading campanula (*C. poscharskyana*) and the late-flowering purple *Clematis viticella* 'Etoile Violette', which will eventually grow through the viburnum. Ivies feature here again – the soft yellow 'Buttercup', 'Parsley Crested', with lovely curly leaves which take on a rich bronzy tone in winter, and the curly 'Irish Lace' – the latter two planted as ground cover under the viburnum, which will also help disguise the inspection cover. The ivies are evergreen, of course, and along with the other evergreen shrubs – hebes, euphorbias, *Viburnum davidii*, *Choisya ternata* and privet honeysuckle (*Lonicera pileata*) – will make the garden attractive in winter, too. Around the front door there's another rose, the scented 'Madame Alfred Carrière' which is happy in a north-facing spot, and, for scent, a honeysuckle, *Lonicera* × *americana*. To fill the inevitable initial gaps between the permanent plants, Jane chose apricot and pale blue violas, creamy-white and lime-green tobacco plants (*Nicotiana*) and a peach-coloured nasturtium, 'Tip Top Apricot'. The ivies in the troughs are two used as ground cover in the garden – the curly-edged 'Parsley Crested' and the variegated, deeply dissected ivy 'Sagittifolia Variegata', which has a lovely lacy effect.

No 23

The Japanese influence in Pam's garden showed clearly in the choice of plants like the mountain pine (*Pinus mugo*) and the wine-red Japanese maple (*Acer palmatum* 'Crimson Queen'). Although the maple needs a shady spot, its new foliage also needs shelter from frost and icy winds in late spring. On paper, it was probably too exposed in Pam's garden for it, but it was one of the plants on which Jane thought it worth taking a chance. Since this garden relied largely on foliage for its colour, Jane chose to mix the deep wine-red of the acer, *Heuchera micrantha* 'Palace Purple' and the small bun-shaped barberry (*Berberis thunbergii* 'Atropurpurea Nana') with gold variegated spindle (*Euonymus fortunei* 'Emerald 'n' Gold'), golden variegated bamboo (*Pleioblastus auricomus*), the plain golden creeping Jenny (*Lysimachia nummularia* 'Aurea'), the golden sedge grass (*Carex hachijoensis* 'Evergold') and the plantain lily (*Hosta* 'Gold Standard'). There was a little plain green, too, like the juniper (*Juniperus* 'Emerald Spreader'), the lovely, fern-like elder (*Sambucus nigra* 'Laciniata') with finely dissected, light green leaves, and the small round leaves of the climber *Akebia quinata*. She also included some of the curious black grass (*Ophiopogon planiscapus* 'Nigrescens'). By the house, for scent, she planted the winter-flowering Christmas box (*Sarcococca hookeriana digyna*) and for summer the climbing rose 'Golden Showers'. The other main flower colours were smoky purples and deep reds – the clematis 'Gipsy Queen', the viola 'Bowles' Black', bugle (*Ajuga reptans* 'Atropurpurea') and wine-red tobacco plants (*Nicotiana*). For the ivies in the troughs, Jane chose the popular gold variegated 'Goldheart' and a variety called *Hedera hibernica* 'Gracilis' which takes on a bronzy purple tint in winter.

No 24

Pauline's favourite colours were soft pinks, blues, mauves, whites – and so that was what Jane focused on. The rose round the door was 'New Dawn', bearing scented, blush-white flowers all summer, with a later-flowering clematis – the large purple-flowered 'Jackmanii' – climbing through it. The feature shrub is an apple, again grown on a dwarfing rootstock but this time it's 'Lord Lambourne'. It'll be pollinated by the apple trees in No 21.

For more scent, Jane chose the little-leaved lilac (*Syringa microphylla* 'Superba'), which has scented pink flowers in early summer and again from late summer until autumn, and the butterfly bush (*Buddleia davidii*). She chose a small cultivar – 'Nanho Blue' – with deep violet-blue flowers, from mid-summer through to autumn, the same colour almost as the salvia (*S. × sylvestris* 'May Night'). Hardy fuchsias are excellent for a small space, since either the frost cuts them down to ground level or you do so in the spring. Jane chose two – the beautiful *F. magellanica* 'Alba' with masses of tiny, pale pink flowers for months, and *F.m.* 'Versicolor' which has small bright scarlet and purple flowers but is grown primarily for its wonderful smoky cream, pink and sage-green foliage. Its foliage colour blends well with the smoky pink flowers of *Dicentra formosa*, with its lovely grey-green, finely-cut leaves while the white potentilla 'Abbotswood' next to it sets it off beautifully too. For winter interest, there's the evergreen *Viburnum tinus* 'Eve Price' which flowers in late winter/early spring, and, to extend its season of interest, Jane chose another late-flowering clematis, *C. viticella* 'Kermesina', with soft wine-red flowers, to scramble through it. The other evergreen shrub, by the inspection cover, was the low-spreading laurel (*Prunus laurocerasus* 'Zabeliana') with slender, glossy, evergreen leaves and candles of white flowers in spring. As for annuals, Jane chose white and pink busy Lizzies (*Impatiens*) and, for scent, white tobacco plants (*Nicotiana*) near the door. As for the ivies above the garage, here Jane chose the very dark green, curly 'Ivalace' and the bird's-foot ivy 'Pedata', with its slender grey-green leaves.

By late summer, the four gardens really did look as though they'd been there for much much longer than four months. The hard landscaping had lost its 'just been laid' look, and the plants had filled out to such an extent that it wasn't possible to squeeze anything else in. The trees and shrubs were still very small, of course, but the perennials and the bedding plants we'd used to fill the gaps had done their job of providing more or less instant impact for the first season or so superbly well. All the owners were delighted with their gardens – even Pam had grown not just to tolerate the gravel but to love the way it looks, especially after we used it to mulch the beds as well. They'd clubbed together to extend the automatic watering system from the troughs controlled from Phil and Karen's house. The gardens continue to give great pleasure not only to the owners but to passers by. There have been nothing but favourable comments, though the one question people always ask is how they manage to drive over the plants in the drives. The very healthy, clearly non-crushed state of all the plants is the best answer there is!

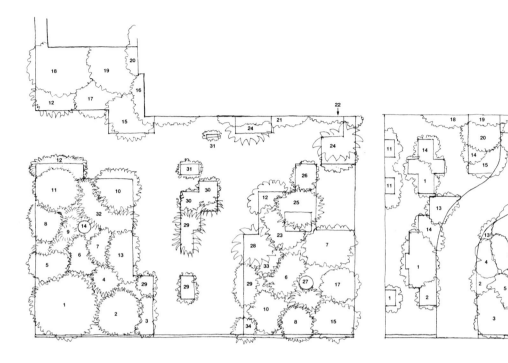

Number 21

1 *Choisya ternata*; 2 *Rosmarinus* 'Miss Jessopp's Upright'; 3 *Viola* 'Huntercombe Purple'; 4 *Crocosmia* 'Lucifer'; 5 *Berberis verruculosa*; 6 *Campanula persicifolia*; 7 *Anemone* × *hybrida* 'Honorine Jobert'; 8 *Lavandula* 'Hidcote'; 9 *Festuca glauca*; 10 *Nepeta* 'Six Hills Giant'; 11 *Potentilla* 'Primrose Beauty'; 12 *Stachys byzantina*; 13 *Salvia officinalis*; 14 Apple 'Discovery'; 15 *Brachyglottis* 'Sunshine'; 16 *Clematis* 'Bill Mackenzie'; 17 *Potentilla* 'Sunset'; 18 *Rosa rugosa* 'Alba'; 19 Existing variegated elder; 20 *Parthenocissus henryana*; 21 *Rosa* 'Kathleen Harrop' and *Clematis* 'Perle d'Azur'; 22 *Hedera helix* 'Green Ripple'; 23 *Hedera helix* 'Glacier'; 24 *Hosta* 'Royal Standard'; 25 *Juniperus horizontalis* 'Hughes'; 26 *Viola* 'Moonlight'; 27 Apple 'Egremont Russet'; 28 *Hosta sieboldiana* 'Elegans'; 29 *Helianthemum*; 30 *Thymus* 'Pink Chintz'; 31 *Thymus* 'Doone Valley'; 32 *Hemerocallis* 'Golden Orchid'; 33 *Hemerocallis* 'Stella de Oro'; 34 *Juniperus squamata* 'Blue Carpet'; Troughs on flat roof: *Hedera helix* 'Green Ripple', *Hedera helix* 'Glacier'; **Additional planting**: White busy Lizzies and tobacco plants.

Number 22

1 *Alchemilla mollis*; 2 *Campanula poscharskyana*; 3 *Hebe rakaiensis*; 4 *Potentilla* 'Daydawn'; 5 *Euphorbia wulfenii*; 6 *Rosa* 'Buff Beauty'; 7 *Lonicera pileata*; 8 *Hemerocallis* 'George Cunningham'; 9 *Clematis viticella* 'Alba Luxurians'; 10 *Hedera helix* 'Parsley Crested'; 11 *Hedera helix* 'Sagittifolia Variegata'; 12 *Viburnum plicatum* 'Mariesii'; 13 Variegated apple mint; 14 *Vinca minor* 'Atropurpurea'; 15 *Astrantia* 'Sunningdale Variegated'; 16 *Choisya* 'Aztec Pearl'; 17 *Lonicera* × *americana*; 18 *Rosa* 'Madame Alfred Carrière'; 19 *Clematis viticella* 'Etoile Violette'; 20 *Viburnum davidii*; **Additional planting**: cream and lime green nicotiana; nasturtium; in troughs on roof: *Hedera helix* 'Parsley Crested'; *Hedera helix* 'Sagittifolia Variegata'.

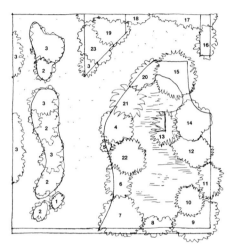

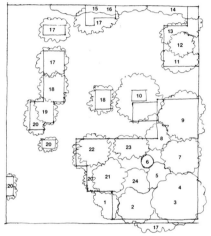

Number 23

1 *Ajuga reptans* 'Atropurpurea';
2 *Lysimachia nummularia*; *Lysimachia nummularia* 'Aurea' mixed; 3 *Ajuga reptans* 'Atropurpurea'; 4 *Berberis thunbergii* 'Atropurpurea Nana'; 5 *Carex hachijoensis* 'Evergold'; 6 *Ophiopogon planiscapus* 'Nigrescens'; 7 *Salvia officinalis* 'Icterina'; 8 *Viola* 'Bowles' Black'; 9 *Nandina domestica* 'Firepower'; 10 Existing conifer; 11 *Cotoneaster dammeri*; 12 *Pleioblastus auricomus*; 13 *Juniperus horizontalis* 'Emerald Spreader'; 14 *Pinus mugo*; 15 *Acer palmatum* 'Crimson Queen'; 16 *Lamium maculatum* 'Aureum'; 17 *Akebia quinata*; 18 *Rosa* 'Golden Showers'; 19 *Sarcococca hookeriana* 'Digyna'; 20 *Heuchera* 'Palace Purple'; 21 *Hosta* 'Gold Standard'; 22 *Sambucus laciniata*; 23 *Euonymus fortunei* 'Emerald 'n' Gold'; **Additional planting**: White busy Lizzies; Dark red nicotiana; Purple violas; Ferns between rocks; Troughs on roof: *Hedera helix* 'Gracilis'; *Hedera helix* 'Goldheart'.

Number 24

1 *Salvia officinalis* 'Purpurascens';
2 *Hebe rakaiensis*; 3 *Viburnum tinus* 'Eve Price'; 4 *Clematis viticella* 'Abundance'; 5 *Hemerocallis* 'Bonanza'; 6 Apple 'Lord Lambourne'; 7 *Potentilla* 'Abbotswood'; 8 *Acanthus spinosus*; 9 *Fuchsia magellanica* 'Versicolor'; 10 *Prunus laurocerasus* 'Zabeliana'; 11 *Sedum* 'Ruby Glow'; 12 *Fuchsia magellanica* 'Alba'; 13 *Viola* 'Huntercombe Purple'; 14 Existing ivy; 15 *Rosa* 'New Dawn'; 16 *Clematis* 'Jackmanii'; 17 *Alchemilla mollis*; 18 *Ajuga reptans*; 19 *Campanula poscharskyana*; 20 *Viola labradorica*; 21 *Buddleia davidii* 'Nanho Blue'; 22 *Syringa microphylla* 'Superba'; 23 *Salvia* 'May Night'; 24 *Dicentra* 'Luxuriant'; In troughs on roof: *Hedera helix* 'Pedata'; *Hedera helix* 'Ivalace'; **Additional planting**: White nicotiana and white, mauve and pink busy Lizzies.

The modern town houses in five years' time

TREES

Apple (*Malus domestica*)
The three varieties 'Discovery', 'Egremont Russet' and 'Lord Lambourne' are all grown on an M 106 rootstock. It's not the smallest by any means, but it produces compact trees that don't need staking and are good on poor soils.
Approx. height and spread: 3–4 × 3 m (10–13 × 10 ft).

CLIMBERS

Akebia quinata
An unusual shade-tolerant climber with a bronzy tint to the young leaves, which are semi-evergreen in mild areas. It has curious, small, brownish flowers in late April followed by purplish fruits. It's very vigorous, and can be used over an arch or up trees.
Approx. height: 10 m (33 ft).

Clematis
The large, summer-flowering 'Gipsy Queen' has single violet-purple flowers from July to September. 'Jackmanii' has single dark purple flowers from July onwards. 'Perle d'Azur' is also very free-flowering with sky-blue flowers from June to August.
Approx. height and spread: 3 × 1 m (10 × 3 ft).
C. 'Bill Mackenzie' has yellow lantern flowers in late summer. *C. viticella* flowers from July to October. 'Kermesina' is a soft wine-red; 'Alba Luxurians' has slightly twisted white petals and 'Etoile Violette' is more vigorous and free-flowering, with dark purple flowers.
Approx. height and spread: 3–4 × 1.5 m (10–12 × 5 ft).

Ivy (*Hedera helix* and *H. hibernica*)
Plain green ivies are bone-hardy and very shade-tolerant, while varieties with variegated or yellow leaves need more light and tend to be less hardy.
'Buttercup' has butter-yellow leaves in a sunny spot.
Approx. height and spread: 2 × 2.5 m (6 ft 6 in × 8 ft).
'Glacier' is silvery grey-green with cream margins.
Approx. height and spread: 3 × 2 m (10 × 6 ft).
'Goldheart' has dark green diamond-shaped leaves with vivid yellow centres but it is not suitable for ground cover.
Approx. height and spread: 4 × 4 m (13 × 13 ft).
H. hibernica 'Gracilis' turns bronze-purple in winter and is not suitable for ground cover.
Approx. height and spread: 5 × 3 m (16 × 10 ft).

'Green Ripple', with very pointed lobes and prominent light green veins, is good for ground cover or against a low wall.

Approx. height and spread: 1.2 × 1.2m (4 × 4ft).

'Irish Lace' or 'Koniger's Auslese', with densely borne, very pointed five-lobed leaves, is a good ground-cover ivy.

Approx. height and spread: 1.2 × 1m (4 × 3ft).

'Ivalace' has very glossy leaves that are crimped at the edges.

Approx height and spread: 1 × 1.2m (3 × 4ft).

'Manda's Crested' has soft, mid-green leaves which can become coppery in very cold weather. 'Parsley Crested' is light green with leaves crested at the edges like parsley, as its name implies.

Approx. height and spread: 3.5 × 3.5m (12 × 12ft).

'Pedata', the bird's-foot ivy, has grey-green leaves, and isn't suitable for ground cover.

Approx height and spread: 4 × 3m (13 × 10ft).

'Sagittifolia Variegata' has deeply cut variegated leaves and is not suitable for ground cover.

Approx height and spread: 1.2 × 1m (4 × 3ft).

Honeysuckle (*Lonicera* × *italica* or × *americana*)

Many of this family will grow in any soil in sun or semi-shade, and this very free-flowering variety has fragrant yellow flowers flushed with purple all summer.

Approx. height and spread: 7 × 7m (23 × 23ft).

Roses

R. 'Golden Showers' This rather stiff upright rose, best suited to a pillar or narrow section of wall, has pale gold, scented, double flowers through summer and autumn.

Approx. height and spread: 2–3 × 2.5m (6ft 6in–10 × 7ft).

R. 'Kathleen Harrop' Very fragrant, double, pale pink flowers are borne in summer on thornless arching stems.

Approx. height and spread: 2.5 × 2m (8 × 6ft).

R. 'Madame Alfred Carrière' This has masses of white, very fragrant flowers from mid-summer to autumn and, while it's happy on a north wall, it's more likely to reach its full size in full sun.

Approx. height and spread: 5.5 × 3m (18 × 10ft).

R. 'New Dawn' Palest blush-white, sweetly scented, double flowers in clusters are borne almost continuously on long stems. It will do well on a north wall but won't reach much more than half its potential size.

Approx. height and spread: 5 × 5m (16 × 16ft).

CONIFERS

Juniper (*Juniperus horizontalis*)
'Emerald Spreader' is a very low-growing wide-spreading conifer, making a 10 cm-(4 in)-thick mat with vivid green, needle-like, aromatic leaves.
Approx. height and spread: 10 cm × 2–3 m (4 in × 6–10 ft).
J.h. 'Hughes' is another low-growing juniper, not as prostrate as 'Emerald Spreader', and this time with layers of silvery foliage.
Approx. height and spread: 20–30 cm × 1.2 m (8 in–1 ft × 4 ft).

Mountain pine (*Pinus mugo*)
This naturally gnarled-looking conifer with long, leathery, green needles in pairs and small, brown cones eventually makes a large, open shrub.
Approx. height and spread: 3–5 × 5–8 m (10–15 × 15–25 ft).

SHRUBS

Maple (*Acer palmatum* 'Crimson Queen')
A superb foliage shrub that needs protection from late spring frosts and strong sunlight. It has very finely dissected leaves in deep wine-red, with good autumn colour. While it prefers neutral to acid soil, it will tolerate alkaline soil if there's sufficient moisture.
Approx. height and spread after five years: 75 cm × 1 m (2 ft 6 in × 3 ft).

Barberry (*Berberis*)
B. thunbergii 'Atropurpurea Nana' has red-purple leaves through spring and summer and colours to an intense orange-red in autumn.
Approx. height and spread: 45 × 60 cm (18 in × 2 ft).
B. verruculosa is slow-growing, with dark, glossy, evergreen leaves, small, bright yellow flowers in the spring and blue-black fruits later. A good shrub for dry shade and exposed sites.
Approx. height and spread: 1.5 × 1.5 m (5 × 5 ft).

Senecio (*Brachyglottis* 'Sunshine')
It has felted grey leaves and in mid-summer is covered with clusters of bright yellow daisy flowers. It can sprawl if left unchecked, so cut it back hard after flowering to keep it compact.
Approx. height and spread after five years: 75 × 75 cm (2 ft 6 in × 2 ft 6 in).

Butterfly bush (*Buddleia davidii*)
All buddleias do well on any soil and in full sun or light shade. See page 34. *B.d.* 'Nanho

Blue' has short clusters of deep blue flowers and narrow grey-green leaves but is half the size of most buddleias. Cut it back hard in early spring to keep it small and improve its flowering performance.

Approx. height and spread after five years: 1.5 × 1.5 m (5 × 5 ft).

Mexican orange blossom (*Choisya ternata*)

An attractive evergreen shrub with aromatic, glossy, mid-green leaves and clusters of fragrant white flowers in late spring/early summer and often again in late summer. It will grow anywhere from full sun to deep shade and will tolerate most soils. If it gets too big, cut it back and it will soon regenerate.

Approx. height and spread after five years: 2 × 2 m (6 × 6 ft).

The new, smaller *C.* 'Aztec Pearl' has distinctive, finely cut foliage and pink buds which open to white. It flowers for weeks in spring and often repeats in late summer.

Approx. height and spread after five years: 1.5–2 × 1.2–1.5 m (5–6 × 4–5 ft).

Cotoneaster dammeri

An evergreen ground-hugger, with glossy small leaves and white flowers in June and round, brilliantly red berries later, it tolerates most soil types and sun or shade, and is ideal for carpeting banks and disguising inspection covers!

Approx. height and spread after five years: 5–7.5 cm × 1.2 m (2–3 in × 4 ft).

Spindle (*Euonymus fortunei* 'Emerald 'n' Gold')

Another invaluable evergreen ground-cover shrub for exposed places, its glossy dark green leaves have bright yellow margins.

Approx. height and spread after five years: 60 cm × 1 m (2 × 3 ft).

Hardy fuchsia (*Fuchsia magellanica*)

F.m. 'Versicolor' has small, red and purple flowers and lovely, smoky, variegated foliage in shades of sage-green, cream and pink. *F.m* 'Alba' has flowers that are palest pink, almost white, and fresh green foliage on elegant arching stems. They grow in any well-drained soil and in sun or part-shade.

Approx. height and spread after five years: 1 × 1 m (3 × 3 ft).

Hebe (*Hebe rakaiensis*)

This has bright green oval leaves and small dense spikes of white flowers in early summer, and forms a neat round bush. It prefers full sun and a well-drained soil but will tolerate shadier conditions.

Approx. height and spread after five years: 30 × 75 cm (1 ft × 2 ft 6 in).

Juniper (*Juniperus horizontalis* 'Hughes')

A carpeting juniper with soft grey-green foliage.

Approx. height and spread after five years: 30 cm × 1.2 m (1 × 4 ft).

J. squamata 'Blue Carpet' has vivid blue leaves.

Approx. height and spread after five years: 20 cm × 2 m (8 in × 6 ft).

Lavender *(Lavandula angustifolia* 'Hidcote')

Lavender does best in full sun and well-drained soil. The neat, compact *L.a.* 'Hidcote' has thick spikes of the deepest violet-blue flowers in mid-summer.

Approx. height and spread: 45 × 45 cm (18 × 18 in).

Privet honeysuckle *(Lonicera pileata)*

An evergreen shrub with stiff branches which fan out in layers and masses of small, glossy leaves. Since it will grow in deep shade under trees, it's useful for gound cover in difficult situations.

Approx. height and spread after five years: 40 cm × 1.2 m (15 in × 4 ft).

Sacred bamboo *(Nandina domestica* 'Firepower')

This evergreen bamboo-like dwarf shrub has leaves which are orange-red when young, light green in summer and scarlet in autumn. It prefers a moist but well-drained soil and a sheltered sunny spot.

Approx. height and spread after five years: 45 × 75 cm (18 in × 2 ft 6 in).

Shrubby cinquefoil *(Potentilla fruticosa)*

Very useful, tough, but attractive little shrubs, these have flowers in shades of white, yellow, orange, flame and pink. 'Abbotswood' has pure white flowers and greyish foliage; 'Daydawn' has creamy peach-pink flowers which hold their colour in sunlight. They both reach only two-thirds the average size. 'Primrose Beauty' has soft primrose-yellow flowers with deeper centres and greyish foliage while 'Sunset' has orange flowers flecked with brick red.

Approx. height and spread after five years: 75 × 75 cm (2 ft 6 in × 2 ft 6 in).

Cherry laurel *(Prunus laurocerasus* 'Zabeliana')

This low-growing spreading form of the cherry laurel makes good cover for open positions, on banks or under trees.

Approx. height and spread after five years: 1 × 3 m (3 × 10 ft).

Roses

R. 'Buff Beauty' is a hybrid musk rose with apricot-buff flowers, pleasantly scented, and glossy, dark green foliage. It flowers profusely in summer, and then less freely in autumn.

Approx. height and spread: 1.2 × 1.2 m (4 × 4 ft).

Rugosa roses are instantly recognizable for their stems covered densely with small

prickles and distinctive wrinkled foliage. They are bone-hardy, disease-resistant and grow well on thin soils. *R. rugosa* 'Alba' has single white flowers in summer and autumn, followed by large, tomato-like hips.
Approx. height and spread: 1–2 × 1–2 m (3–6 × 3–6 ft)

Rosemary (*Rosmarinus officinalis* 'Miss Jessopp's Upright')
A vigorous and upright form of the common rosemary, with blue flowers in late spring. It likes well-drained soil and a sunny position.
Approx. height and spread: 2 × 2 m (6 × 6 ft).

Sage (*Salvia officinalis*)
S.o. 'Purpurascens' has blue flowers in spring and leaves that are purple when young, then grey-purple, then green-purple, while 'Icterina' has golden variegated foliage and is reckoned to be the hardiest of the variegated sages.
Approx. height and spread after five years: 75 cm × 1 m (2 ft 6 in × 3 ft).

Elder (*Sambucus nigra* 'Laciniata')
This has delightful, finely divided, fern-like leaves. It needs a third of the oldest wood pruned out each year, or you can cut it back hard to keep it small.
Approx. height and spread after five years (unpruned): 3 × 2 m (10 × 6 ft).

Christmas box (*Sarcococca hookeriana digyna*)
Highly scented flowers in winter make this modest plant valuable in the garden. It grows in sun or shade and any fertile soil.
Approx. height and spread after five years: 25 × 30 cm (10 in × 1 ft).

Little-leaved lilac (*Syringa microphylla* 'Superba')
A delicate version of the ordinary lilac, with oval leaves and small pink flowers in late spring and again in late summer, it is slow growing, ideal for lovers of lilac with very small gardens. It isn't fussy about soil type and will grow in sun or part-shade.
Approx. height and spread after five years: 60 × 45 cm (2 ft × 18 in).

Viburnums
Viburnum davidii A spreading evergreen shrub which makes a low mound of dark green, leathery, deeply veined foliage with small white flowers in spring. There are male and female plants and, if you plant at least one of each, the female will produce attractive turquoise berries.
Approx. height and spread after five years: 75 × 75 cm (2 ft 6 in × 2 ft 6 in).
Lacecap viburnum (*Viburnum plicatum* 'Mariesii') A mature *V.p.* 'Mariesii' is a stunning sight in early summer with its tiered horizontal branches covered with flat, white, lacecap flowers. The foliage also has lovely autumn colour.

Approx. height and spread after five years: 1.5 × 2 m (5 × 6 ft).
Vibernum tinus 'Eve Price' This compact form of 'Laurustinus' has pink buds opening to white star-shaped flowers in winter.
Approx. height and spread: 2.5 × 2.5 m (8 × 8 ft).

PERENNIALS

Bear's breeches (*Acanthus spinosus*)
This variety has spikier leaves. See page 120.

Bugle (*Ajuga reptans*)
See page 21.

Lady's mantle (*Alchemilla mollis*)
This tough plant, with fan-like fresh green leaves and tiny lime-green flowers, grows anywhere, sun or shade, in any soil.
Approx. height and spread: 50 × 50 cm (20 × 20 in).

Japanese anemone (*Anemone* × *hybrida* 'Honorine Jobert')
This has single white flowers with conspicuous yellow stamens in late summer and early autumn.
Approx. height and spread: 1 m × 60 cm (3 × 2 ft).

***Astilbe* 'Bronce Elegans' or 'Bronze Elegance'**
Like all astilbes, this has plume-like heads of tiny flowers – rich purple rather than bronze – and deeply cut leaves. They do best in damp rich soil and partial shade.
Approx. height and spread: 30 × 30 cm (12 × 12 in).

Masterwort (*Astrantia* 'Sunningdale Variegated')
This has greenish-white flowerheads tinged with pink all summer while its lobed leaves are variegated with cream and yellow.
Approx. height and spread: 60 × 45 cm (2 ft × 18 in).

Campanulas
Peach-leaved campanula (*Campanula persicifolia*) This has spires of blue bell-shaped flowers from June to August. Moist soil and light shade suit it best, but it also flourishes on chalk and in full sun.
Approx. height and spread: 30–75 × 30 cm (1 ft–2 ft 6 in × 1 ft).
Campanula poscharskyana A rampant spreader that puts out vigorous runners covered with small mauve-blue bell-flowers in summer, but it can easily be kept under control if

they are pulled off in handfuls. Invaluable for dry shade.
Approx. height: 10–15 cm (4–6 in); spread: indefinite.

Sedge (*Carex hachijoensis* 'Evergold')
An evergreen tuft-forming grass with narrow yellow-striped leaves.
Approx. height and spread: 20 × 15–20 cm (8 × 6–8 in).

Crocosmia 'Lucifer'
This has stiff sword-like leaves and flame-red flowers in mid-summer for weeks.
Approx. height and spread: 60 × 25 cm (2 ft × 10 in).

Dicentra formosa
Worth having for its finely divided grey-green leaves as well as its smoky pink flowers in early summer.
Approx. height and spread: 45 × 30 cm (18 × 12 in).

Spurge (*Euphorbia wulfenii*)
An architectural evergreen with whorls of blue-green leaves on tall stems and heads of lime-green flowers in spring.
Approx. height and spread: 1.2 × 1.2 m (4 × 4 ft).
E. griffithii 'Fireglow' has orange-red flowers in early summer, and red-tinged stems and leaves as well.
Approx. height and spread: 1 m × 50 cm (3 ft × 20 in).

Sheep's fescue (*Festuca glauca*)
This evergreen ornamental grass has blue-grey leaves and flowering stems in summer.
Approx. height and spread: 15 × 23 cm (6 × 9 in).

Rock roses (*Helianthemum* cultivars)
Low-growing summer-flowering evergreens that produce masses of saucer-shaped flowers in white, yellow, red and pink over mats of grey foliage.
Approx. height and spread: 10–15 × 60 cm (4–6 in × 2 ft).

Day lily (*Hemerocallis*)
The showy lily-like flowers last for only a day but appear in succession over a number of weeks in summer. *H.* 'George Cunningham' has apricot-coloured flowers; *H.* 'Golden Orchid' is deep orange-yellow; *H.* 'Bonanza' is pearly apricot, and the dwarf *H.* 'Stella de Oro' has grassy green leaves and bright yellow flowers with an orange throat continue for months.
Approx. height and spread: variable – 30 cm–1 m × 45–75 cm (12 in–3 ft × 18 in–2 ft 6 in).

Heuchera micrantha 'Palace Purple'
Grown mainly for its purple leaves, it also has small sprays of whitish flowers in early summer.
Approx. height and spread: 45 × 45 cm (18 × 18 in).

Plantain lily (*Hosta*)
H. 'Gold Standard' has broad gold leaves finely edged with dark green and pale violet flowers in mid-summer. *H*. 'Royal Standard': see page 80. *H. sieboldiana* 'Elegans' is one of the largest hostas with striking waxy blue leaves and very pale lilac almost white flowers.
Approx. height and spread: 60 cm–1 m × 1–1.5 m (2–3 × 3–5 ft).

Dead nettle (*Lamium maculatum*)
See page 80.

Creeping Jenny (*Lysimachia nummularia*)
This evergreen ground-cover plant with bright yellow cup-shaped flowers in summer can become rampant in moist conditions. *L.n.* 'Aurea' has yellow leaves and is less invasive.
Approx. height and spread: 2.5 cm × 1 m (1 in × 3 ft).

Apple mint (*Mentha suaveolens* 'Variegata')
The soft, woolly, mid-green leaves splashed with white smell of apples. It grows anywhere, but can be invasive if it's really happy.
Approx. height and spread: 30 × 60 cm (1 × 2 ft).

Catmint (*Nepeta* 'Six Hills Giant')
It has soft grey-green foliage and spikes of purple-blue flowers in early summer and again in autumn if cut back after the first flowering.
Approx. height and spread: 60 × 60 cm (2 × 2 ft).

Ophiopogon planiscapus 'Nigrescens'
Grown for its distinctive, black, grass-like leaves, it has lilac flowers in summer, followed by black berries.
Approx. height and spread: 23 × 30 cm (9 × 12 in).

Pleioblastus auricomus
An evergreen, slow-spreading bamboo with purple stems and broad yellow and green striped leaves. In a moist but free-draining soil and sunny position it can be invasive, so chop it back.
Height: 75 cm–1.2 m (2 ft 6 in–4 ft); spread: indefinite.

Salvia (*Salvia* × *sylvestris* 'May Night')

Dramatic spikes of violet-blue, freely borne in late summer.
Approx. height and spread: 50 cm–1 m × 45 cm (20 in–3 ft × 18 in).

Ice plant (*Sedum* 'Ruby Glow')
This has bluish-green fleshy leaves and wide heads of ruby-red flowers in mid- to late-summer.
Approx. height and spread: 20 × 20 cm (8 × 8 in).

Lamb's lugs (*Stachys byzantina*)
Most forms are silver, but *S.b.* 'Primrose Heron' is golden-leaved, with magenta flowers.
Approx. height and spread: 40 × 60 cm (15 in × 2 ft).

Thyme (*Thymus* 'Doone Valley' and 'Pink Chintz')
See page 89.

Lesser periwinkle (*Vinca minor* 'Atropurpurea')
This variety has plum-purple tubular flowers in early spring, instead of the usual blue, over small, glossy, evergreen leaves.
Approx. height: 15 cm (6 in); spread: indefinite.

Pansy, Violet (*Viola*)
V. 'Bowles' Black' has tiny, deep violet, almost black flowers from spring to autumn. *V.* 'Huntercombe Purple' has a profusion of soft violet flowers from spring through to late summer. *V.* 'Moonlight': see page 61. *V. labradorica* (now *V. riviniana*; Purpurea group) has small, purple, heart-shaped leaves and light violet flowers – a very good plant in dry shade where it doesn't spread quite so vigorously.
Approx. height and spread: 5–10 × 10–15 cm (2–4 × 4–6 in).

ANNUALS

Busy Lizzie (*Impatiens*)
Produces masses of flowers in white, shades of pink, mauve, coral and red for months in sun or deep shade.
Approx. height and spread: 15 × 15 cm (6 × 6 in).

Tobacco plant (*Nicotiana*)
Sweetly scented tubular flowers in shades of white, lime-green and red.
Approx. height and spread: 60 × 30 cm (2 × 1 ft).

Nasturtium (*Tropaeolum majus*)
See page 81.

THE CORNER GARDEN

*F*or many people, a corner house seems a very attractive proposition, because it usually has a bigger garden than the other houses in the street. And once they've bought their corner, they often find that they do indeed have more land – it wraps around the house – but, since most front gardens are divided up by the drive, what they wind up with is two separate gardens, on different sides of the house, facing different directions, that don't really relate to each other at all.

That was certainly true of our corner plot. The long narrow strip down the side of the house had always been a problem, and was now just rather poor grass with a large lilac in the middle, taking most of the light. But in this instance the problem was even more complicated. The house was one of a pair of suburban semis, built in 1932, and set at an angle across the corner. The owners – Joyce Wilding on the left who'd moved in with her mother when the house was brand-new, and Jack and Norah Chapman on the right who'd lived there nearly forty years – soon became such firm friends that they took down the post-and-chain boundary between their gardens many years ago, and since then have treated it as one space. It would have looked very odd, therefore, if we'd tackled only Joyce's garden, so we followed their lead and treated the two front gardens as one.

In the main area of the garden there were narrow borders with spring bulbs and bedding down the sides of each drive, one along the front of the house under the bay windows and a few roses along the fence. The rest was laid mainly to grass – even the owners insisted that it was so full of moss and weeds that calling it 'lawn' would be pitching it a bit high! The houses face due north, so the area under the windows is in shade for most of the day, but the rather spongy, mossy nature of the grass suggested that poor drainage rather than shade alone might be the main cause. The soil is light, and slightly on the acid side of neutral, so plants like rhododendrons do well.

They all enjoyed gardening. Jack spent a lot of time in the greenhouse or working on his vegetable patch, and neither Joyce nor Nora could imagine being without at least a little area of garden. But they were all in their mid-70s and simply couldn't do as much as they once did – Nora has arthritis and was awaiting a hip replacement. And, sensibly, they were also thinking ahead to a time when they'd be able to do even less.

What they wanted at the front was a garden that was attractive all year round, but that largely took care of itself. Joyce was keen to keep at least a bit of lawn, though they all agreed that in the existing gardens there was too much of it, it needed too much looking after and, even then, it never looked good. Jack also felt that the garden looked very flat and could do with some height.

Nora wanted lots of flowers – roses, scented if possible, and clematis – and her favourite colours are pinks, blues and silvers. Joyce loves bright colours particularly, while yellow is a special favourite of Jack's. And given that Jack and Nora celebrated their golden wedding in May 94, it seemed only right that there should be some horticultural celebration of that event.

The design

Penelope Smith was immediately excited by the possibilities of our corner plot. While she could see the problems – the rather sunless, north-facing aspect, the poor state of the lawn, the flatness of the garden, the fact that the house seemed rather isolated from the garden, and the extra bit of garden tucked away round the side – she could see solutions to them all.

The first thing she wanted to do was make a very generous bed – about 1.5m (5ft) deep – up against the house, following the lines of the two bay windows, and fill them with mainly evergreen, shade-tolerant shrubs, some variegated, to bring some much-needed brightness into the shadiest part of the garden. She edged the bed with a low box hedge to contain the planting and emphasize the formal lines. Although it would need trimming twice a year to keep its lines razor-sharp, an annual trim would be good enough, and both Jack and Joyce thought that with a bit of help from specially designed equipment they could cope well enough with that.

They are such good friends that the traffic between the two front doors is considerable and, of course, the shortest, most direct route – also favoured by tradesmen – was across the grass. So Penny put in a broad path between the two front doors, again following the shape of the bays. Where the line of the bed went in between the two bays, the other side of the path mirrored it, going outwards and creating a broader area in the middle, where she suggested siting four terracotta pots filled with bedding.

Although the house bricks were a lovely warm orange-red colour, Penny felt on reflection that a large area of them in the garden, especially close to the emerald green of the lawn, would be rather too dominant. So instead she chose narrow brick paviours in a softer brindle shade, to be laid in a herringbone pattern with the 'V' of the pattern going widthways across the path, rather than lengthways along it, taking your eye back and forth across the path and making it seem wider than it is.

Penny, like Joyce, was keen to keep a small area of lawn in the garden since there are broad grassy verges in the streets and she felt it would tie the garden in with its surroundings. The shape of the bays gave her the idea of a small, central, octagonal lawn, edged with a mowing strip of the same brick as the path. That makes it extremely quick and easy to mow and, if in future years even that small area of lawn becomes too much to care for, it can easily be replaced with the same bricks or gravel.

On Jack and Norah's side of the lawn, Penny put a small brick-paved area to take a seat – since it would be surrounded on three sides by shrubs, it would be both sheltered and private. She used the same brick paviours, only this time laid them in a basket-weave pattern. Although Joyce had thought it unlikely that she would ever sit out in the garden, Penny felt that once she saw Jack and Norah enjoying their seat, she might change her mind, so she put in a small paved area for her too, facing due west and catching the evening sun. If Joyce doesn't sit out, then it's the perfect place for some large containers.

To get immediate height in the garden, Penny chose to put three very simple obelisks about 2m (6ft) high among the planting and grow climbers like clematis and honeysuckle up them. The obelisks, which are easy to make yourself or can be bought in kit form, matched the low, squared-trellis boundary fence. They were all keen to keep this fence because, first, it was in the original style of the estate's fences and, second, it was relatively new so it would have been a waste of money to replace it. Penny decided to stain it and the obelisks an attractive shade of deep blue-green called 'Neptune'.

To solve the problem of how to link the narrow side area of garden to the rest of it, Penny put in a gravel path with a brick edge, leading from Joyce's side of the new lawn up to her drive, and then, in a continuation of the same line, from the far side of the drive to a much smaller brick octagon halfway down the side garden, with a large planted container in the centre. A pair of conifers placed at the bend of the path took your eye over to that side of the lawn, and the line of the new path made sure it didn't stop at the drive but carried on into the side garden. The repeated octagon was another strong visual link between the two areas, as was her plan to use some of the same plants in both.

In this aerial 'before' shot (*left*), our pair of corner gardens look very flat indeed. Three months later this shot, taken from the front door on the left (*below*) shows how easy it is to achieve instant height in a garden with standard roses and simple obelisks, and how much better it looks.

Building the garden

The original plan had been to leave the existing drives but coat them with a thin layer of resinated gravel which would look more attractive. It looks like gravel but, since it is bonded with resin, it doesn't move around. Once work got under way, though, we found that the levels weren't right and the drives were too high, so they were dug up, the levels adjusted, then they were reconcreted and coated with resinated gravel.

Since the path between the two houses was for pedestrian traffic only, it was laid on screeded sand, edged with a very strong but light and easy-to-fix polymer edge restraint, which is held in place with 20cm (8in) steel pins. Obviously, if you are using these pins, it is vital to check first where service pipes and cables are laid. They should be considerably more than 20cm below the surface, but this really is a case of better safe than sorry!

The same paviours were laid on concrete as a mowing edge for the octagonal lawn. Before we could lay the lawn, though, we needed to solve the drainage problem. The soil was very boggy 10–15cm (4–6in) down in that central area. The most likely explanations were that the garden dipped considerably in the middle so that water drained into it from the rest of the garden, and possibly that the soakaway for the central downpipe on the front of the houses wasn't soaking away as efficiently as it once had done. So we raised the level of the soil a good few centimetres and dug in some grit to improve the drainage.

Then we relaid the lawn, using turf. It is more expensive than making a new lawn from seed, but it would have been fiendishly difficult to seed a lawn inside an octagonal brick mowing strip.

Once the turf was laid, we put the sprinkler on for a couple of hours, and then made sure that it was watered little and often – every day if there was no rain – until the turf had rooted into the soil. That can take anything between a few days and a few weeks, depending on how moist and warm the soil is, but you can tell when it's happened because the grass stops looking flat and sad and starts to stand up and look a much fresher green.

Planting

As the garden is by no means a standard shape, there are several different aspects which largely dictate the choice of plants. The patch round the side, for instance, is east-facing and shaded by the house on one side and street trees on the other for most of the day. The bed along the front of the house faces due north and so gets hardly any sun at all, while the area by the fence gets enough sun in summer for roses and lavender to do well.

The other main considerations in the choice of plants were low maintenance, meaning permanent planting which took care of itself, and colour all through the year. That indicated a large proportion of evergreens, some with variegated leaves to add welcome brightness in the cold dreary winter months.

The openness of the garden meant that wind was a factor Penny had to take into account, especially on Jack and Norah's side of the garden, so between their drive and the back of their seat, she planted tough wind-resistant evergreen shrubs, like *Elaeagnus × ebbingeii*, *Mahonia × media* 'Charity' and Portugal laurel (*Prunus lusitanica*). In the case of the elaeagnus, we went for the largest specimens we could find because, although they were expensive, they were the first line of defence and we really needed to get some shelter established quickly for the rest of the garden and for the residents.

As for instant height in the garden, in addition to the obelisks, Penny chose a small tree – the silver weeping pear (*Pyrus salicifolia* 'Pendula') – and a couple of standard roses, 'Iceberg' in this instance, chosen for its fragrant pure white flowers and long flowering period.

In the very shady border under the bay windows, she chose the climbing hydrangea (*H. anomala petiolaris*) to scramble up the wall, and some tough shade-loving evergreens – like the spring-flowering camellia *C.* 'Alba Plena' with double white flowers, the invaluable *Euonymus fortunei* 'Emerald Gaiety', *Skimmia japonica* 'Rubella' and a very attractive variety of tough elephant's ears, *Bergenia* 'Wintermärchen'. There had been a blue hydrangea by Joyce's front door for as long as she could remember, but the current incumbent was very old, woody and clearly long past its best, so we replaced it with *Hydrangea macrophylla* 'Mariesii Perfecta' (formerly 'Blue Wave'), and planted one on Jack and Norah's side for good measure. The soil is acid enough to keep it blue-flowered and not turn it pink.

The bed was edged with dwarf box (*Buxus sempervirens*) and in each corner of the broader central area of the path Penny planted a golden shrubby honeysuckle (*Lonicera nitida* 'Baggesen's Gold'), and clipped them into spheres. By the side of each front door she opted for another evergreen, firethorn (*Pyracantha* 'Orange Glow'), with white flowers in early summer and bright orange-red berries in the autumn, which can be trained very easily to follow the lines of the door.

For the sunnier border along the fence, Penny chose shrubs like lavender, the sun rose (*Cistus*), hebes like 'Purple Queen' and the compact, bun-shaped 'Red Edge', and fast-growing tree mallow (*Lavatera*) – in this case, a new white-flowered one called 'Ice Cool', which is slightly less rampant than the pink-flowered varieties. There were roses, too, of course – the superb yellow English rose, 'Graham Thomas', for Jack and Norah, and for Joyce, the soft pink, strongly fragrant 'Heritage'. For scent, as well as the lavender and the roses, we planted herbs like rosemary, marjoram (*Origanum*) and sage (*Salvia*).

The herbaceous plants in that border were mainly pink, mauve and white, with clumps of Japanese anemones, penstemons – 'White Bedder', the deep purple 'Sour Grapes' and the wine-red 'Garnet' – bear's breeches (*Acanthus mollis*), ice plant (*Sedum* 'Autumn Joy') and catmint (*Nepeta*). The foliage was in smoky colours – blues, like the huge-leaved *Hosta sieboldiana* 'Elegans'; purples, like *Heuchera micrantha* 'Palace Purple'; and silver, like lamb's lugs (*Stachys byzantina*).

Against two of the obelisks we planted sweetly scented evergreen Japanese honey-suckle (*Lonicera japonica* 'Halliana'), with the blue-flowered clematis 'Perle d'Azur' growing through it, while on the third we trained *Solanum jasminoïdes* 'Album' with morning glory (*Ipomoea hederacea*). Through the newly stained deep blue-green fence, we trained the white everlasting pea (*Lathyrus latifolius* 'Albus').

As for containers, Penny suggested filling the four terracotta pots on the wider central area of the path with shade-tolerant bedding like pale salmon pelargoniums and pale blue lobelia. For the small octagon in the side garden, we opted for a barrel, stained the same colour as the trellis and filled with hostas (*H. sieboldiana* 'Elegans') for huge impact. Given the amount of green-fingered crime these days, we decided to fill the bottom half of the barrel with rubble, making it impossible for anyone to lift it without a crane! We also tried a new security system, developed for the art market, consisting of a number of small tags, which can be attached to pots or benches or even lawn mowers and which if moved even very slightly will set off the alarm in the base unit indoors.

To keep maintenance to the bare minimum, even in the early days, we covered the soil with a woven membrane which allows water to permeate, but prevents it evaporating too quickly and stops weeds from germinating. To make life simpler, we put the largest shrubs in first, then laid the membrane round them. The smaller shrubs and herbaceous plants were planted through X-shaped cuts in the membrane, which to be honest is very fiddly, but the long-term reward – practically no weeding, ever – is well worth the effort. Once all the plants were in, we mulched with chunky bark – since the garden is somewhat exposed to the wind, we wanted something reasonably hefty that wouldn't blow around too easily.

By September, the garden was looking lovely and remarkably mature. Despite their earlier reservations about having a bench and sitting out there, the lovely weather in June and July meant they were sitting out most days, particularly in the evenings, and thoroughly enjoying the garden. It has proved extremely easy to look after with no weeding, just a bit of deadheading – 'pottering' which Jack and Joyce both enjoy – and

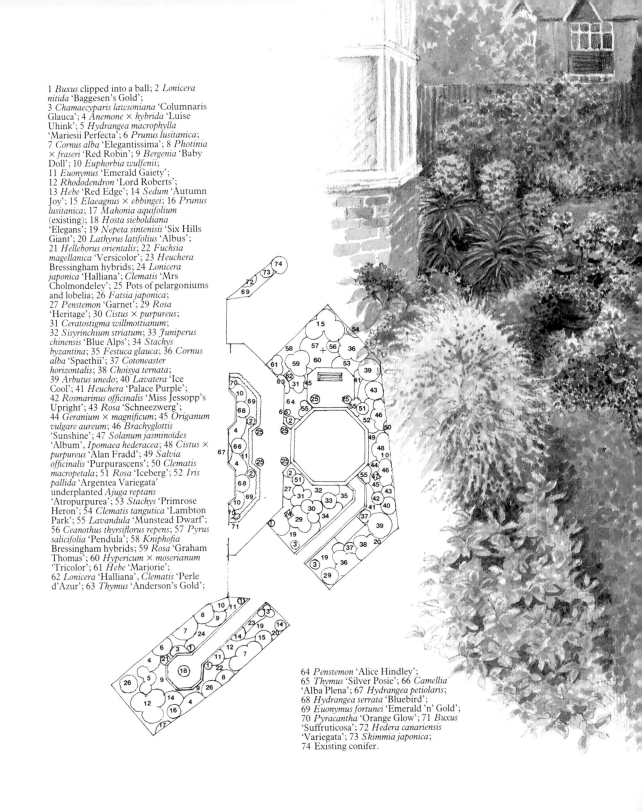

1 *Buxus* clipped into a ball; 2 *Lonicera nitida* 'Baggesen's Gold';
3 *Chamaecyparis lawsoniana* 'Columnaris Glauca'; 4 *Anemone* × *hybrida* 'Luise Uhink'; 5 *Hydrangea macrophylla* 'Mariesii Perfecta'; 6 *Prunus lusitanica*; 7 *Cornus alba* 'Elegantissima'; 8 *Photinia* × *fraseri* 'Red Robin'; 9 *Bergenia* 'Baby Doll'; 10 *Euphorbia wulfenii*;
11 *Euonymus* 'Emerald Gaiety';
12 *Rhododendron* 'Lord Roberts';
13 *Hebe* 'Red Edge'; 14 *Sedum* 'Autumn Joy'; 15 *Elaeagnus* × *ebbingei*; 16 *Prunus lusitanica*; 17 *Mahonia aquifolium* (existing); 18 *Hosta sieboldiana* 'Elegans'; 19 *Nepeta sintenisii* 'Six Hills Giant'; 20 *Lathyrus latifolius* 'Albus';
21 *Helleborus orientalis*; 22 *Fuchsia magellanica* 'Versicolor'; 23 *Heuchera* Bressingham hybrids; 24 *Lonicera japonica* 'Halliana'; *Clematis* 'Mrs Cholmondeley'; 25 Pots of pelargoniums and lobelia; 26 *Fatsia japonica*;
27 *Penstemon* 'Garnet'; 29 *Rosa* 'Heritage'; 30 *Cistus* × *purpureus*;
31 *Ceratostigma willmottianum*;
32 *Sisyrinchium striatum*; 33 *Juniperus chinensis* 'Blue Alps'; 34 *Stachys byzantina*; 35 *Festuca glauca*; 36 *Cornus alba* 'Spaethii'; 37 *Cotoneaster horizontalis*; 38 *Choisya ternata*;
39 *Arbutus unedo*; 40 *Lavatera* 'Ice Cool'; 41 *Heuchera* 'Palace Purple';
42 *Rosmarinus officinalis* 'Miss Jessopp's Upright'; 43 *Rosa* 'Schneezwerg';
44 *Geranium* × *magnificum*; 45 *Origanum vulgare aureum*; 46 *Brachyglottis* 'Sunshine'; 47 *Solanum jasminoïdes* 'Album', *Ipomaea hederacea*; 48 *Cistus* × *purpureus* 'Alan Fradd'; 49 *Salvia officinalis* 'Purpurascens'; 50 *Clematis macropetala*; 51 *Rosa* 'Iceberg'; 52 *Iris pallida* 'Argentea Variegata' underplanted *Ajuga reptans* 'Atropurpurea'; 53 *Stachys* 'Primrose Heron'; 54 *Clematis tangutica* 'Lambton Park'; 55 *Lavandula* 'Munstead Dwarf';
56 *Ceanothus thyrsiflorus repens*; 57 *Pyrus salicifolia* 'Pendula'; 58 *Kniphofia* Bressingham hybrids; 59 *Rosa* 'Graham Thomas'; 60 *Hypericum* × *moserianum* 'Tricolor'; 61 *Hebe* 'Marjorie';
62 *Lonicera* 'Halliana', *Clematis* 'Perle d'Azur'; 63 *Thymus* 'Anderson's Gold';

64 *Penstemon* 'Alice Hindley';
65 *Thymus* 'Silver Posie'; 66 *Camellia* 'Alba Plena'; 67 *Hydrangea petiolaris*;
68 *Hydrangea serrata* 'Bluebird';
69 *Euonymus fortunei* 'Emerald 'n' Gold';
70 *Pyracantha* 'Orange Glow'; 71 *Buxus* 'Suffruticosa'; 72 *Hedera canariensis* 'Variegata'; 73 *Skimmia japonica*;
74 Existing conifer.

The corner garden in
five years' time

with the soaker hose taking care of watering the borders, just putting the sprinkler on the lawn every couple of days, and cutting it once a week. Jack, Norah and Joyce were all delighted with the garden which had turned out to look even better than they had imagined from the initial plans. They all loved the fact that there was always something different to look at – as one shrub or clump of perennials finished flowering there was always something else just starting to flower.

The garden was also greatly admired by neighbours – indeed Jack was told by one of them that it really enhanced the whole estate – and by people from further afield who'd heard about it and came to see for themselves. By next summer, Jack said, they fully expected to be serving cream teas!

TREES

Silver weeping pear (*Pyrus salicifolia* 'Pendula')
This small tree eventually forms a dense mound of long, willow-like, silvery foliage, covered in white down when it first unfurls.
Approx. height and spread after five years: 2.5 × 2 m (8 × 6 ft).

CLIMBERS

Clematis
C. 'Perle d'Azur' has sky-blue flowers from mid-summer until well into the autumn.
Approx height and spread: 4 × 4 m (13 × 13 ft).
C. × *jackmanii* has large purple flowers in late summer.
C. orientalis, a late flowering one, has lantern-shaped yellow flowers, followed by silvery seedheads.
Approx. height and spread: 3 × 1.5 m (10 × 5 ft).

Ivy (*Hedera helix* 'Glacier' and *H.h.* 'Green Ripple')
See page 96.

Climbing hydrangea (*Hydrangea anomala petiolaris*)
An excellent, self-clinging climber for a north wall, this has heart-shaped leaves and flat, white, lacecap hydrangea flowers in early summer.
Approx. height and spread: 6 × 6 m (20 × 20 ft).

Morning glory (*Ipomoea hederacea*)
See page 39.

Everlasting pea (*Lathyrus latifolius* 'Albus')
This has white pea-flowers in summer and early autumn.
Approx. height and spread: 2–3 × 1.5–2 m (6–10 × 5–6 ft).

Japanese honeysuckle (*Lonicera japonica* 'Halliana')
See page 33.

SHRUBS

Wormwood (*Artemisia* 'Powis Castle')
This non-flowering form is grown for its feathery, aromatic, silver-grey foliage. It is evergreen but looks scruffy in the spring, so cut it back hard.
Approx. height and spread: 1 × 1.2 m (3 × 4 ft).

Senecio (*Brachyglottis* 'Sunshine')
See page 98.

Box (*Buxus sempervirens* 'Suffruticosa')
See page 34.

Camellia **'Alba Plena'**
A lovely variety with double white flowers and mid-green, glossy, evergreen leaves.
Approx. height and spread after five years: 1 × 1 m (3 × 3 ft).

Shrubby plumbago (*Ceratostigma willmottianum*)
This is an autumn-flowering shrub with brilliant blue flowers and foliage that colours well. The frost may cut it back, but it will regrow.
Approx. height and spread after five years: 60 × 60 cm (2 × 2 ft).

Mexican orange blossom (*Choisya ternata*)
See page 99.

Sun rose (*Cistus × purpureus* 'Alan Fradd')
This one has large white flowers with maroon blotches at the base and bright yellow stamens. Each flower lasts for only one day but there is a succession from early to late summer.
Approx. height and spread: 1.5 × 1 m (5 × 3 ft).

Dogwood (*Cornus alba* 'Elegantissima')
This has elegant, white-edged, green leaves and bright red stems in winter while *C.a* 'Spaethii' has gold and green variegated leaves and the same sealing-wax-red stems. Cut both back hard each spring for the brightest stem colour. See also page 34.

Elaeagnus × *ebbingei*
This quick-growing evergreen with tough grey-green leaves (which look as though they've been sprayed with gold paint when they first emerge) is an excellent screening shrub with hidden, but fragrant, flowers in late summer. A good windbreak and background shrub.
Approx. height and spread after five years: 1.2 × 1.2 m (4 × 4 ft).

Euonymus
E. fortunei 'Emerald 'n' Gold': see page 99. *E.* 'Emerald Gaiety' is a more subtle variety with white variegations which turn pink in very cold weather.

Euphorbia characias wulfenii
See page 103.

False castor-oil plant (*Fatsia japonica*)
A first-class architectural evergreen for shade, with large, deeply lobed, glossy green leaves.
Approx. height and spread after five years: 2 × 2 m (6 × 6 ft).

Fuchsia magellanica 'Versicolor'
See page 99.

Shrubby veronica (*Hebe*)
H. albicans 'Red Edge' is a low-growing hebe with white flowers and blue-grey foliage edged with red.
Approx. height and spread: 30 × 75 cm (1 × 2 ft 6 in).
H. 'Purple Queen' is a taller variety with long spikes of deep purple flowers and purple-green to purple leaves from mid-summer until early autumn.
Approx. height and spread: 1 × 1 m (3 × 3 ft).
See also page 99.

Lacecap hydrangea (*Hydrangea macrophylla* 'Mariesii Perfecta')
This used to be known as 'Blue Wave', and is blue on acid soils and pink on alkaline soils.
Approx. height and spread after five years: 1 × 1.2 m (3 × 4 ft).

Chinese juniper (*Juniperus chinensis* 'Kuriwao Gold')
A broad-spreading gold juniper.
Approx. height and spread after five years: 1 × 1.2 m (3 × 4 ft).

Lavender (*Lavandula angustifola* 'Munstead')
A compact and long-flowering lavender with dense blue spikes.

Tree mallow (*Lavatera thuringiaca* 'Ice Cool')
This new small mallow has large white flowers, freely borne from summer to the frosts. It's not as vigorous or as hardy as the pink forms, so give it a sheltered spot.
Approx. height and spread: 1.2 × 1.2 m (4 × 4 ft).

Shrubby honeysuckle (*Lonicera nitida* 'Baggesen's Gold')
This evergreen with tiny golden leaves is useful either for clipping as a hedge or topiary, or leaving to make a layered shrub.
Approx. height and spread after five years: 1 × 2 m (3 × 6 ft).

Mahonia × media 'Charity'
An outstanding evergreen for shade, with its whorls of jagged deep green leaves and large yellow scented flowers in winter.
Approx. height and spread after five years: 1.5 × 1 m (5 × 3 ft).

Photinia × fraseri 'Red Robin'
The new growth on this evergreen, produced from late autumn onwards, is brilliant red and ages to bronze in late spring and summer.
Approx. height and spread after five years: 1.5 × 2 m (5 × 6 ft).

Portugal laurel (*Prunus lusitanica*)
Another valuable screening evergreen with glossy dark green leaves, candles of scented white flowers in spring and red berries in autumn.
Approx. height and spread after five years: 1 × 1 m (3 × 3 ft).

Firethorn (*Pyracantha* 'Orange Glow')
A wall shrub with white flowers in late spring, orange-red berries in autumn and small, glossy, evergreen leaves all year.
Approx. height and spread after five years: 1.5 × 1 m (5 × 3 ft).

Rosemary (*Rosmarinus* 'Miss Jessopp's Upright')
A tall variety of the family. See page 77.

Roses
R. 'Blanche Double de Coubert': see page 57.
R. 'Graham Thomas' is one of the best new English roses, with double flowers of rich yellow on a slightly arching plant and good foliage. *R.* 'Heritage' has lovely soft pink flowers with an old rose scent with a note of lemon. It soon forms a good bushy shrub and flowers all summer.
Approx. height and spread: 1.2 × 1.2 m (4 × 4 ft).
R. 'Iceberg' is first class as a shrub or a standard, with large trusses of almost pure white,

double flowers all summer, carried over crisp, shiny, pale green leaves.
Approx. height and spread of shrub: 1.2 × 1.2 m (4 ft × 4 ft).

Sage (*Salvia officinalis* 'Purpurascens' group)
See page 101.

Skimmia japonica 'Rubella'
This evergreen flowering shrub has dark leathery leaves and spikes of scented white flowers, deep red in bud, in spring. This is a male form, so there are no berries.
Approx. height and spread after five years: 40 × 40 cm (15 × 15 in).

PERENNIALS

Bear's breeches (*Acanthus mollis*)
This has shiny, jagged, bright green, semi-evergreen leaves and spikes of mauve and white hooded flowers in summer.
Approx. height and spread: 1 m × 45 cm (3 ft × 18 in).

Japanese anemone (*Anemone × hybrida* 'Luise Uhink')
Excellent in shade, it has pure white bowl-shaped flowers on tall stems in late summer above clumps of dark green, deeply cut leaves.
Approx. height and spread: 1 m × 45 cm (3 ft × 18 in).

Elephant's ears (*Bergenia* 'Wintermärchen')
This neat bergenia has bright rose-pink flowers in spring and small, spoon-shaped, rich green leaves, which are red when young.
Approx. height and spread: 30 × 30 cm (1 × 1 ft).

Campanula portenschlagiana
A prostrate evergreen, making dense mats of small ivy-shaped leaves with masses of open-bell blue-mauve flowers in summer. It can be invasive, but is easily chopped back.
Approx. height: 15 cm (6 in); spread: indefinite.

Erysimum 'Bowles' Mauve'
The perennial wallflower with grey-green foliage and mauve flowers for months in spring and summer.
Approx. height and spread: 45 × 45 cm (18 × 18 in).

Bronze fennel (*Foeniculum vulgare* 'Purpureum')
See page 36.

Geranium × magnificum
This one forms clumps of almost scalloped leaves with clusters of cup-shaped violet-blue flowers in July and August.
Approx. height and spread: 45 × 45 cm (18 × 18 in).

Heuchera micrantha 'Palace Purple'
See page 104.

Hosta sieboldiana 'Elegans'
See page 104.

Catmint (*Nepeta* 'Six Hills Giant')
See page 104.

Wild marjoram (*Origanum vulgare*)
This forms mats of aromatic, oval, green leaves and clusters of tiny mauve flowers on wiry stems in summer.
Approx. height and spread: 45 × 45 cm (18 × 18 in).

Penstemon
P. 'Garnet' has clear garnet-red flowers, while *P.* 'Sour Grapes' bears flowers the colour of unripe purple grapes, a mixture of green, mauve and purple, over a long season. *P.* 'White Bedder' has startlingly white trumpets on bushy plants from early to late summer.
Approx. height and spread: 45–75 × 30–60 cm (18–30 in × 1–2 ft).

Ice plant (*Sedum* 'Autumn Joy')
This plant is attractive all year with fleshy pale green leaves in spring and large flat flowerheads that start green in summer, turn pink in late summer and rusty-red in winter. Butterflies love it.
Approx. height and spread: 60 × 60 cm (2 × 2 ft).

Lamb's lugs (*Stachys byzantina*)
See page 105.

Horned violet (*Viola cornuta*)
This has deep lavender flowers like large violets throughout the summer.
Approx. height and spread: 20 × 20 cm (8 × 8 in).

ANNUALS

Busy Lizzie (*Impatiens*)
See page 105.

Tobacco plant (*Nicotiana*)
See page 105.

THE COMMUNAL GARDEN

You could say that most front gardens are shared gardens in the sense that most houses are owned by couples, and that means you've got two people whose views have to be taken into account. If they have similar ideas about how the garden should be used, and about how it should look, that's fine. But if they both have different and equally strong opinions, it can be very difficult to reach a satisfactory compromise.

In some instances, though, there are not just two people to please. Lots of us now live in flats, either in large old houses which have been divided up, or in small purpose-built blocks, and so any garden has to be shared. In some cases, back gardens are divided up into tiny plots, one for each flat, but with a front garden that isn't a realistic option. And then of course there is the car. Even if you allow just one car per flat – and the reality is that many couples have a car each – that can add up to an awful lot of cars to be accommodated in the front garden.

Our communal garden belonged to a large late-Victorian house, to which another wing had been added in Edwardian times, and which had been divided up some time ago into five flats. To the right of the front door there was a large bay window with a tall, pointed gable above it and a conservatory to the left of it. The newer part blended in well in terms of the brick colours but it was rather plain compared to the older part.

The garden ran the width of the house – 15m (50ft) – but was only 6m (20ft) deep at most, so it was rather shallow. The boundary was a white painted ranch-style fence – quite wrong for the period of the house. It was also broken in parts and some of the posts were rotting, so its days were numbered.

Although the house faced due south, it was a rather shady garden because of all the trees along the front. At the entrance to the drive was a huge copper beech, probably planted when the house was built. They are magnificent trees but, once they are in leaf, they cast perhaps the deepest shade of any deciduous tree and it's extremely difficult to get anything to grow underneath them. On the plus side here, the tree had been well pruned over the years, with some of the lower branches removed and the crown thinned to allow more light to penetrate.

Running along the fence was a narrow, slightly wavy border, edged on the garden side with bricks. It was sparsely planted with an assortment of shrubs and trees, like laurel and spotted laurel (*Aucuba japonica*) and a large mature holly tree. Some of them, like a few other scrubby hollies and a laburnum, were self-seeded and some had been badly hacked in the past. It also had its fair share of large tree stumps.

On the sunnier south-facing side of the garden, along the house walls, was a very narrow bed only about 50cm (20in) wide, where various occupants had planted shrubs, roses and bulbs, but not many had thrived, perhaps because they'd been planted too close to the house walls where the soil was extremely dry.

But undoubtedly the dominant feature of the garden was the huge expanse of gravel right down the middle, allowing parking for six or seven cars and what the others called 'the kebab van' – a large white trailer in which one of their number kept his moto-cross motorbikes.

The overall impression was of a car park, with the house cut off from what little real garden there was, and certainly the two did nothing to complement each other. Between them, the residents owned eight cars (plus the kebab van) and, while there were four garages at the back of the house, they were used for storage. There was room to park three or four cars round there, too, but people usually parked at the front.

They had decided, though, that they would really like a proper front garden, and not a car park. They accepted, too, that in theory they would be jointly responsible for its upkeep, but they knew from their experience with the back garden that it probably wouldn't work very well in practice since they all have demanding jobs and have very active social lives. So a garden that required the minimum of maintenance was essential.

Apart from the shared problem of parked cars, though, the residents all had slightly different problems with the front garden. For Frank Reilly and Lesley Hay on the ground floor to the right of the front door, for instance, the other major problem was the trees blocking out much of the light through their front windows. Their sitting room had the magnificent bay window but they rarely sat in it because it was so shady. What they wanted from the new garden was a way of minimizing the impact of the parked cars, and Frank was particularly keen on structure – good evergreen 'bones' in the garden to look at all year round.

For Kari and Laurence Koonin and their daughter Sophie, who lived on the ground floor on the other side of the front door, the problem was different again. The conservatory was part of their flat, but while the tall trees blocked out some of their light, the lower planting wasn't dense enough to screen them from the road and provide enough privacy to allow use of the conservatory on a regular basis. So they wanted a bit more privacy and a much more attractive garden.

For Jane Goldstein and Neil Anderson on the first floor, the trees, and the giant copper beech in particular, were a godsend because they screened the new development over the road, and filtered out much of the noise from the street. Their main gripe about the garden was that it was dull and uninspiring and what they wanted, Jane particularly, was lots of bright colours. For Mike Fredriksen, owner of two cars (and the kebab van), the main priority was an attractive garden that took care of itself, since what with work and his hobbies, there was no time over for gardening.

For garden designer Nicholas Roeber, the garden presented a real challenge. There was a number of pluses – the house itself was attractive with a long stretch of south-facing wall, there was space to play with, and there were some mature trees and shrubs to provide a framework. But there was also a considerable number of minuses. The ranch-style fence was one, so was the ungenerous border along the front of the house, and the very dense shade cast by the copper beech. But top of the problem list for him, too, was the need for so much parking space. Since everyone agreed that it would be impossible to have any kind of decent garden *and* keep the same amount of parking space, they reached a compromise, and agreed to park four cars round the back, leaving Nick to find room at the front for three or four cars . . . and the trailer.

In fact the trailer posed an interesting challenge: although not that many people have to park trailers in their front gardens, there are thousands of caravan owners with similar problems. If Nick could find a solution to that one, he would earn the gratitude not only of our other residents, but of neighbours all over Britain!

The design

Clearly the first thing to be done was to solve the parking problem. Nick's initial thoughts were to use the rather dead area in the far left-hand corner of the garden, adjoining the road, as designated parking. But that would have meant leaving a large area of gravel right down the middle of the garden to provide access to it. So in the end he decided to make the parking area in front of the newer part of the house, just inside the entrance, leaving about two-thirds of the space free to become a proper garden.

Before (*left, above*) our communal garden does look like a car park. Now (*left, below*), it looks like a
proper garden with much more generous planting areas while the new path focuses attention
on the most attractive part of the house.

Above: The simple railings and gate add the finishing touch, restoring to the house the elegance it must
have had in its prime.

127

His next thought was that the most striking part of the house – the large bay window and the steep gable above it – was never really seen in all its glory, since you approached the house at a very sharp angle, from the side. He also felt that a line from the pavement, half-way along the fence, to the front door was the obvious 'desire line', too. We knew it was, having witnessed the postman a few days earlier hopping over the fence there and cutting across the border! So Nick decided to put in a central brick path leading straight towards the central bay and the gable, but then pivoting at a small brick octagon, two-thirds of the way in, and curving left towards the front door. He'd noticed a band of patterned brick on the front of the house with square blue header bricks interspersed among the red so, using cheaper modern clay paviours instead of bricks, he picked up the same pattern for the path – always an excellent way of forging the link between house and garden.

To the right of the path, from the octagon back towards to the copper beech, Nick created a large planting area for shade-tolerant shrubs and woodland ground-cover plants, with lots of spring-flowering bulbs which would make the best of the extra light and moisture available to them when the leaves were off the tree.

To the left of the path, he created another generous border of shrubs and ground cover to sweep in a broad curve right round to the far end of the conservatory. He kept the large holly, but pruned it into a more formal conical shape, moved a couple of the large spotted laurels and a large, healthy clump of Solomon's seal (*Polygonatum* × *hybridum*) and took out a number of other trees and large shrubs, including the laburnum. Nick knows from experience just how poisonous laburnum is, having seen a friend's dog eat a small sprig of it last year and die within twenty-four hours, and so it's really not a good tree where there are small children or pets.

In the roughly circular area he had created in the process, in front of the conservatory, he decided to make a lawn, using a specially formulated grass mixture that will tolerate shade and won't require a lot of mowing.

As for the front of the house, having created the beginnings of symmetry with the new central path, he wanted to enhance it and blend the newer wing with the rest of the house. He did it by fixing three white metal rose arches over the three ground-floor windows, to balance the conservatory and pick up the ogee shape of its windows on the other side. They would be covered with climbers like roses, honeysuckle and clematis, and would also provide a visual distraction from the parked cars for Frank and Lesley as they looked out of their bedroom window. Since the area on either side of the new path had been cleared of some taller shrubs – some of them replanted elsewhere in the garden – and the area of the large holly had been reduced, it meant that not only did they get much more light in through the bay window but a far more attractive view out of it too.

Broadly following the line of the bay, Nick created a much more generous bed around it and along the front of the house. He decided to leave the area in front of the conservatory clear of planting to draw attention to its very attractive lines, but put in a few stepping stones for easy access to the far end of the garden.

The ranch-style fencing clearly had to go, and railings seemed the most obvious replacement for them. It was highly likely that the house did have railings originally which had been taken away to be melted down during the last war. Nick chose very simple railings, 1·65m (5½ft) high, with gate posts to echo the decorative detail of the porch.

And then, of course, there was the kebab van. Nick's first thought had been to tuck it away on a piece of redundant land between the side of the conservatory and the hedge at the far end of the garden. But it needed not just an area of hardstanding on which to park but an even larger one to manoeuvre in and out, and since that would have taken up a huge amount of space, it wasn't practical. Finally he decided that the only place for it was the area of dead space in the far left-hand corner of the garden, where he had originally considered parking the cars. It would have its own entrance direct from the road, so it wouldn't have to come through the garden, and could be screened from the house and the rest of the garden, too. Since it's not only large but white and therefore very visible, we decided to hide it in a tunnel, which would eventually be covered with greenery.

Building the garden

The first job to be done was to clear gravel from the areas that were to be garden. To make life simpler, the top soil for the new lawn was dumped in heaps down the far end of the garden before the new path was laid, since it would have been impossible to back a lorry up there afterwards.

For the path, we laid a mixture of square and rectangular clay paviours in a pattern to match the decorative band of bricks on the house, on a bed of screeded sand. The fact that the paviours were small and came in different shapes made it easier to lay the curve from the octagon to the front door, but even so some slivers of brick had to be cut to fit with an angle grinder. Once the edgings were cemented in place, silver sand was brushed into the joints and the paviours were compacted down with a vibrating plate. We used reproduction Victorian rope-top edging tiles, which obviously were just right for the period of the house, and we chose the charcoal-grey ones since they picked up the colour of the square headers in the path perfectly.

Once the cement had set, we tackled the lawn, first raking out the piles of top soil to make it as level as possible and to get rid of as many stones as we could. Then we compacted it, treading every centimetre of it with our heels – a job where many feet make light work. It is tiring, hard on the calf muscles if you do it right, and you do feel extremely silly, but it really is the only way of doing the job properly. If you use a roller, you flatten the peaks but leave the troughs untouched.

The next step was to feed it – a handful of Growmore per square metre – and then to rake it again very carefully, just to open up the top centimetre of soil enough to make a hospitable seedbed. It was also the last chance to get rid of any little dips, by crouching down every couple of metres and looking along the ground. Broader hollows didn't matter so much – it's the small ones that the mower will just skim over that will give you problems later with weeds and coarse grass. The soil was rather dry, so we gave it a soaking with a sprinkler (which, of course, within the hour brought on the first rain for a week or so). Once the surface of the soil was just drying out, we sowed the seed, a special mixture for shady places at the recommended rate – 50g to the square metre.

Once the seed was sown, we raked it lightly in with a springtined rake. The aim is to cover about half the seed with soil. Birds can be a problem, even though most seed now is treated with a repellant, because they like to have dust baths in the carefully prepared soil. To discourage them, we stuck in a few bamboo canes with strips of kitchen foil tied round the top which move in the wind, make a noise and of course flash when the light catches them. I suspect, though, that Prince, the black house cat, was a much more effective deterrent.

We dug over the rest of the borders, which was hard work since there were lots of roots from trees and shrubs that had gone as well as from those that remained, and in some parts of the garden the soil was quite heavy. We dug in plenty of compost, along with some gravel, to open up the pockets of clay soil, and compost alone to make the areas of sandy soil more moisture-retentive. And since the soil was so poor, we added some other nutrients – fish, blood and bone and bonemeal – to give the plants a boost, short and long term.

We planned to put in a simple automatic watering system – a porous hose, which gently seeps water along its length, woven around the new plants in the shady borders. Since there were beds on both sides of the path, and the last thing we wanted was water seeping gently into its foundations, we laid a short length of ordinary hose under the path as it was being laid, and connected the porous hose to it on either side. That way the whole area could be watered with one turn of the tap.

For the three windows, we bought off-the-peg, easy-to-assemble ogee rose arches, made from nylon-coated metal, plus some extensions, because they had to be taller than the standard size. Since you can only buy them in black, and we wanted ours white to match the conservatory, we rubbed them down with fine sandpaper and then sprayed them with two coats of quick-drying radiator paint. They looked terrific.

For the parking area for the trailer, we used paviours for the hardstanding and then made a tunnel from a series of linked, black plastic-coated arches. It was very tall, with the top already part-hidden by the branches of the surrounding trees, but had we shortened the legs (which would have been very simple to do with a hacksaw), it would have left much more of the structure exposed, and so much more visible. Since we wanted to cover the whole thing in greenery, we fixed special tough black nylon mesh between the uprights, over which climbers like large-leaved Persian ivy (*Hedera colchica* 'Dentata Variegata') or the large-leaved crimson glory vine (*Vitis coignetiae*) would scramble.

Planting

For the front of the house, Nick chose a variety of climbers. For the walls themselves, he chose the lovely scented soft apricot climbing rose 'Meg', which has a major flush of flowers in June but then repeats throughout the rest of the summer, and is vigorous enough to reach up to Jane's and Neil's windows. Over the arches he suggested the late-flowering Dutch honeysuckle (*Lonicera periclymenum* 'Serotina') and the lovely, small, wine-red-flowered *Clematis* 'Madame Julia Correvon'. To help cover ugly drainpipes to the right side of the bay *Magnolia grandiflora*, with its beautiful, huge, creamy, bowl-like flowers up to 25cm (10in) across and very large, glossy, evergreen leaves, was an ideal choice. It eventually makes a very large shrub and works very well with the generous proportions of the house. On the other side of the bay the evergreen clematis, *C. armandii*, with its very fragrant flowers in spring, was a good choice to cover another downpipe.

In the border itself, we planted deep blue, creeping ceanothus, *C. thyrsiflorus repens*, and the vivid magenta sun rose (*Cistus* × *purpureus*) to satisfy Jane's need for hot colours, *Hebe* 'Purple Queen' and, for scent, Rose 'Heritage', daphnes and *Viburnum juddii* for the spring and the little-leaved lilac (*Syringa microphylla* 'Superba') for summer.

On each side of the door, like sentries, we planted two clipped box cones – expensive, but they give the entrance such immediate impact that it's worth spending the money.

On the shady side of the garden, we planted a range of plants that are happy in slightly acid, woodland conditions: camellias like the single white-flowered *C.* 'Devonia', one on either side of the gate, rhododendrons like 'Sappho' and, in my view, the loveliest of all the small ones, *R. yakushimanum*, *Pieris floribunda* 'Forest Flame', and, for ground cover, early-flowering scented shrubs like *Osmanthus* × *burkwoodii* and mahonia, ferns, hellebores, lungwort (*Pulmonaria*), *Tellima grandiflora*, comfrey (*Symphytum*), Siberian bugloss (*Brunnera*), *Pachysandra terminalis*, lesser periwinkle (*Vinca minor*) in white and blue, with taller specimens like the lovely Turk's-cap lilies (*Lilium martagon* 'Album') growing through them. Having clipped one of the small self-sown hollies into what will eventually be an umbrella shape, we planted a clematis, 'Perle d'Azur', to grow through it. Along both sides of the path, we planted evergreen *Hebe rakaiensis*, which grows naturally into a rounded shape and so would provide a slightly formal edging.

To the left of the path, around the big holly, we planted more woodland ground cover and, in a sunnier spot, the late-flowering *Ceanothus* 'Autumnal Blue' along with a mock orange blossom, *Philadelphus* 'Belle Etoile'. Over the tunnel to hide the trailer we planted *Vitis coignetiae*, which has enormous leaves which turn brilliant bonfire colours in autumn, and large-leaved ivy (*Hedera colchica* 'Dentata Variegata').

Once all the plants were in, we laid porous hose around them, and then mulched with a recycled mulch to keep the weeds down and the moisture in. The hose slowly soaks the soil about 7.5cm (3in) each side of it, so it needs to be quite close to the rootball of a plant, and spreading mulch on top not only hides it but acts like a sponge, spreading the water more widely.

By the end of the summer, with the railings in place, the garden really did look like a proper garden, and not a car park with just a few things growing round the edges. The central path had transformed the whole shape of the garden, and really did focus the eye on the most attractive part of the house. The rose arches over the windows of the newer wing, especially as the climbers began to do their job, made a big difference and did link it much more to the older part of the house. Since much of the impact in this garden would come from the planting, rather than from hard landscaping, and since it does take time for shrubs and ground cover plants to mature, it did look a bit sparse in some of the shadier areas under the trees, but even so you could already see that in a year or two, there would be the tapestry of foliage that Nick Roeber had in mind. The climbers we planted to cover the kebab van had just started growing, though obviously it would be a year or two before they covered it completely. Even so, it made the trailer far less obtrusive than it had been before. The owners were all delighted with the transformation. As Laurence Koonin said, it *feels* like being in a lovely garden now, and for the first time in his life, he's become a passionate gardener and loves working out there.

CLIMBERS

Clematis

C. armandii: see page 53.

Spring-flowering *C. macropetala* has masses of long, semi-double, mauve-blue flowers, followed by fluffy seedheads.

Approx. height and spread: 3 × 3 m (10 × 10 ft).

C. 'Ernest Markham', a vigorous late-flowered clematis, has vivid magenta petals and chocolate anthers, while 'Perle d'Azur' has sky-blue flowers.

Approx. height and spread: 3–4 × 3–4 m (10–12 × 10–12 ft).

C. 'Madame Julia Correvon' has flattish, wine-red flowers with twisted petals in summer. *C.v.* 'Alba Luxurians': see page 96.

Approx. height and spread: 3.5 × 3.5 m (11 × 11 ft).

Persian ivy (*Hedera colchica* 'Dentata Variegata')

This has large, cream and grey-green leaves, and needs a little more support initially than most ordinary ivies.

Approx. height and spread: 4 × 4 m (12 × 12 ft).

Early and late Dutch honeysuckle (*Lonicera periclymenum*)

L.p. 'Belgica' blooms early in May and June with deep pink and cream scented flowers, while *L.p.* 'Serotina', with darker flowers, blooms from July to October. Plant them together for a long flowering season.

Approx. height and spread: 4 × 4 m (12 × 12 ft).

Rosa 'Meg'

A climber with almost flat apricot-pink flowers that has its main flush of blooms in June but repeats well throughout the summer.

Approx. height and spread: 4 × 4 m (12 × 12 ft).

Crimson glory vine (*Vitis coignetiae*)

This very vigorous vine has huge leaves which colour brilliantly in autumn.

Approx. height and spread: 12 × 12 m (40 × 40 ft).

SHRUBS

Box (*Buxus sempervirens*)
See page 34.

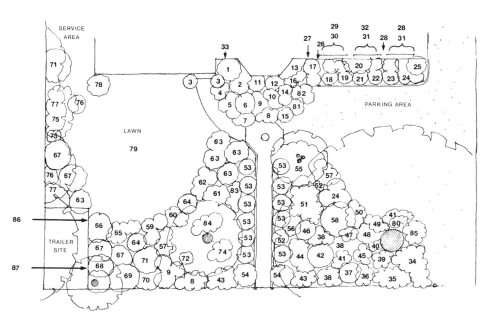

1 *Philadelphus* 'Belle Etoile'; 2 *Choisya ternata*; 3 *Buxus sempervirens*; 4 *Hosta fortunei* 'Albomarginata'; 5 *Sarcococca hookeriana humilis*; 6 *Viburnum × bodnantense*; 7 *Viburnum davidii*; 8 *Acanthus mollis*; 9 *Hebe* 'Purple Queen'; 10 *Hibiscus* 'Blue Bird'; 11 *Hydrangea villosa*; 12 *Syringa microphylla* 'Superba'; 13 *Berberis thunbergii* 'Atropurpurea'; 14 *Rosa* 'Heritage'; 15 *Brachyglottis* 'Sunshine'; 16 *Cistus × purpureus*; 17 *Ceanothus thyrsiflorus repens*; 18 *Salvia officinalis* 'Purpurascens'; 19 *Artemisia* 'Powis Castle'; 20 *Viburnum × burkwoodii*; 21 *Cistus × corbariensis*; 22 *Caryopteris × clandonensis*; 23 *Rosa* 'Queen Mother'; 24 *Skimmia japonica*; 25 *Viburnum tinus*; 26 *Parthenocissus henryana*; 27 *Magnolia grandiflora*; 28 *Rosa* 'Meg'; 29 *Clematis* 'Étoile Violette'; 30 *Lonicera periclymenum* 'Serotina'; 31 *Lonicera periclymenum* 'Belgica'; 32 *Clematis* 'Madame Julia Correvon'; 33 *Clematis armandii*; 34 *Pachysandra terminalis*; 35 *Helleborus orientalis*; 36 *Symphytum rubrum*; 37 Existing rhododendron; 38 *Dicentra eximia*; 39 *Epimedium × rubrum*; 40 *Vinca minor* 'Bowles Variety'; 41 *Heuchera* 'Palace Purple'; 42 *Osmanthus × burkwoodii*; 43 *Bergenia cordifolia*; 44 *Lamium maculatum*; 45 *Polygonatum × hybridum*; 46 Rhododendron; 47 *Hosta tardiana* 'Halcyon'; 48 *Lilium martagon*; 49 *Brunnera macrophylla* 'Variegata'; 50 *Tiarella cordifolia*; 51 *Trachystemon orientalis*; 52 *Galium odoratum*; 53 *Hebe rakaiensis*; 54 *Camellia* 'Devonia'; 55 *Magnolia sieboldii*; 56 *Symphytum grandiflorum*; 57 *Tellima grandiflora* 'Purpurea'; 58 *Ilex aquifolium*; 59 *Potentilla* 'Elizabeth'; 60 *Geranium macrorrhizum* 'Album' 61 *Vinca major* various; 62 *Geranium nodosum*; 63 *Mahonia aquifolium*; 64 *Pieris japonica*; 65 *Symphytum* 'Goldsmith'; 66 *Fatsia japonica*; 67 *Prunus laurocerasus* 'Otto Luyken'; 68 *Camellia* 'Donation'; 69 *Ceanothus* 'Autumnal Blue'; 70 *Viburnum × burkwoodii* 'Park Farm Hybrid'; 71 *Aucuba japonica*; 72 *Helleborus corsicus*; 73 *Elaeagnus × ebbingei*; 74 *Hedera helix*; 75 *Polystichum* 'Herrenhausen'; 76 *Rhododendron* 'Sappho'; 77 *Dryopteris linearis*; 78 *Ilex* with *Clematis* 'Perle d'Azur' growing through it; 79 Naturalized bulbs in lawn; 80 *Euonymus fortunei* 'Emerald Gaiety' 81 *Osmanthus delavayi*; 82 *Persicaria amplexicaule* 'Atrosanguineum'; 83 *Prunella webbiana* 'Loveliness'; 84 *Iris foetidissima*; 85 *Euphorbia robbiae*; 86 *Vitis coignetiae*; 87 *Hedera colchica* 'Dentata Variegata'

The communal garden in five years' time

Camellia

C. 'Devonia' is a fast-growing, upright and bushy cultivar, with single small white flowers and small leaves, bronze when young. *C.* 'Leonard Messel' has large, semi-double, flattish rose-pink flowers and large dark green leaves. All camellias need an acid soil.

Approx. height and spread after five years: 1 × 1 m (3 × 3 ft).

Creeping blue blossom *(Ceanothus thyrsiflorus repens)*

This has rich blue flowers on a spreading mound of small, glossy, evergreen leaves in late spring.

Approx. height and spread after five years: 1 × 2 m (3 × 6 ft).

One of the few late-flowering varieties, *C.* 'Autumnal Blue', has mid-blue flowers in late summer and small evergreen leaves and is one of the hardiest.

Approx. height and spread after five years: 2 × 2 m (6 × 6 ft).

Mexican orange blossom *(Choisya ternata)*

See page 99.

Sun rose *(Cistus × purpureus)*

This has saucer-shaped magenta flowers in mid-summer, and narrow evergreen grey-green leaves.

Approx. height and spread: 1 × 1 m (3 × 3 ft).

Euonymus fortunei 'Emerald Gaity'

See page 118.

Tassel bush *(Garrya elliptica)*

This evergreen is grown primarily for its long grey-green catkins in spring. *G.e.* 'James Roof' has the most spectacular tassels.

Approx. height and spread after five years: 2.5 × 1.5 m (8 × 5 ft).

Hebe 'Purple Queen'

See page 118.

Hebe rakaiensis

See page 99.

Magnolia

M. grandiflora is a spectacular evergreen with large, thick, creamy white, very fragrant, bowl-shaped flowers from late spring to early autumn and very large, glossy, evergreen leaves. It eventually makes a very imposing shrub.

Approx. height and spread after five years: 1.8 × 1 m (5 ft 6 in × 3 ft).

M. wilsonii, the spreading, deciduous member of the family, has hanging, saucer-shaped, white flowers with crimson stamens in late spring/early summer.
Approx. height and spread after five years: 1.5 × 2m (5 × 6ft).

Oregon grape (*Mahonia aquifolium*)
This evergreen shrub has spiky leaves that turn purple-red in winter, and clusters of yellow flowers in spring followed by blue-black fruits in autumn. It's useful ground cover in shade.
Approx. height and spread after five years: 75cm × 1m (2ft 6in × 3ft).
M. japonica, a taller, architectural variety, has long, fragrant spikes of lemon-yellow flowers in the winter, and whorls of long jagged leaves. It's upright when young, but spreads with age.
Approx. height and spread after five years: 1.5 × 1.8m (5ft × 5ft 6in).

Osmanthus × burkwoodii
This bushy evergreen has privet-like dark green leaves and tubular, fragrant, white flowers in early spring.
Approx. height and spread after five years: 2 × 2m (6 × 6ft).

Pachysandra terminalis
A useful evergreen carpeter that's happiest on neutral or acid soil, it has light green leaves and small white flowers in mid spring. It will thrive in deep shade, provided there is enough moisture.
Approx. height and spread after five years: 30cm × 1m (1 × 3ft 3in).

Mock orange blossom (*Philadelphus* 'Belle Etoile')
A medium-sized member of the family, this one has large white flowers with a maroon central blotch.
Approx. height and spread after five years: 1 × 1m (3 × 3ft).

Rhododendron
R. yakushimanum has a long season of interest, with rose-pink buds opening to apple-blossom-pink flowers, slowly fading to white, and very striking leaves which are silver-white with down when they first appear, then really dark green on top, with woolly-brown undersides.
Approx. height and spread after five years: 60 × 60cm (2 × 2ft).
R. 'Sappho' has mauve flower buds opening to pure white with rich purple on the inside. It makes an open, rounded shrub.
Approx. height and spread after five years: 1.2 × 1.5m (4 × 5ft).

The box cones either side of the front door really do draw the eye to it, while
the new lawn provides the perfect foil for both the woodland planting and
the formal lines of the conservatory.

Rosa 'Mutabilis'

This wonderful China rose has masses of single flowers, copper in bud, opening yellow,
fading to pink and then magenta for months in summer. Where it's happy it can get very
large.

Approx. height and spread after five years: 2–3 × 2 m (6–10 × 6 ft).

Sage (*Salvia officinalis* 'Purpurascens' group)
See page 101.

Rose 'Heritage'
See page 119.

Christmas box (*Sarcococca hookeriana humilis*)
This is a smaller, suckering form with the scented white flowers in winter followed by black fruit. See page 101.
Approx. height and spread after five years: 25 × 30 cm (10 in × 1 ft).

Skimmia japonica **'Rubella'**
See page 120.

Little-leaved lilac (*Syringa microphylla* 'Superba')
See page 101.

Irish yew (*Taxus baccata* 'Fastigiata')
This very slow-growing, pillar-like, dark green yew is an excellent accent plant in any planting scheme.
Approx. eventual height and spread: 10 × 4 m (30 × 12 ft).

Viburnum juddii
This has clusters of pink-tinted, round flowers which are highly scented in mid to late spring. Its grey-green leaves may colour in autumn before they fall.
Approx. height and spread after five years: 75 × 75 cm (2 ft 6 in × 2 ft 6 in).

Laurustinus (*Viburnum tinus*)
See page 36.

Lesser periwinkle (*Vinca minor*)
V.m. 'Bowles' Variety' has large, lavender-blue trumpet-flowers above dark glossy green leaves. *V.m.* 'Gertrude Jekyll' has a mass of smaller white flowers and forms very dense ground cover.
Height: 15 cm (6 in); spread: indefinite.

PERRENNIALS

Bear's breeches (*Acanthus mollis*)
See page 120.

Siberian bugloss (*Brunnera macrophylla* 'Hadspen Cream')
This variety has sprays of vivid blue forget-me-not flowers in spring, held above heart-shaped green leaves lightly variegated with deep cream.
Approx. height and spread: 30 × 60 cm (1 × 2 ft).

Male fern (*Dryopteris filix-mas*)
It may be common, but this is a lovely fern with tall, elegantly arching fronds that's good in deep shade.
Approx. height and spread: 1.2 × 1 m (4 × 3 ft).

Euphorbia amygdaloïdes robbiae
See page 36.

Euphorbia characias wulfenii
See page 103.

Geranium macrorrhizum
Superb ground cover for dry shade, this has soft magenta-pink flowers in early summer and aromatic semi-evergreen leaves which colour a little in autumn.
Approx. height and spread: 30 × 60 cm (1 × 2 ft).

Hellebores
Helleborus orientalis: see page 37.
Corsican hellebore (*H. argutifolius* or *corsicus*) has pale, apple-green, hanging flowers in handsome clusters in winter, over dramatic, evergreen leaves that are long and oval with prickly edges.
Approx. height and spread: 60 × 45 cm (2 ft × 18 in).

Hosta fortunei 'Albomarginata'
This hosta has thin-textured mid- to dark green leaves with irregular white margins and violet flowers on tall stems in mid-summer.
Approx. height and spread: 75 cm × 1 m (2 ft 6 in × 3 ft)

Solomon's seal (*Polygonatum* × *hybridum*)
See page 38.

Polypody (*Polypodium vulgare* 'Cornubiense')
This small evergreen fern has highly divided leaves that give a lacy effect and will tolerate drier soil than many ferns.
Approx. height and spread: 25 × 25 cm (10 × 10 in).

Lungwort (*Pulmonaria saccharata* 'Argentea')
This lungwort has long leaves that are almost pure silver, with pink buds opening to blue flowers in early spring.
Height and spread: 25 × 50 cm (10 × 20 in).

Comfrey (*Symphytum grandiflorum*)
This ground-cover plant has spikes of cream tubular flowers in spring and forms weed-suppressing clumps of hairy green leaves.
Height and spread: 25 × 60 cm (10 in × 2 ft).

Tellima grandiflora 'Rubra'
This woodland perennial carries tiny, pinkish, bell-shaped flowers on long stems in spring above low clumps of maple-like leaves.
Approx. height and spread: 60 × 60 cm (2 × 2 ft).

Trachystemon orientalis
This large-leaved, ground-cover plant has short spikes of violet-purple flowers before the leaves early in the year.
Approx. height and spread: 25 cm × 1 m (10 in × 3 ft).

BULBS

Turk's-cap lily (*Lilium martagon* 'Album')
This has small, white, nodding, reflexed flowers in early summer. It's happy in dappled shade or full sun.
Approx. height and spread: 1–1.2 m × 15 cm (3–4 ft × 6 in).

INDEX